A special thanks is given to the family of faith at Shepherd's Fold Baptist Church where these studies were developed, taught, and completed.

Thank you Mrs. Julie Rydberg for the many hours you spent to meticulously read and proof the manuscript.

Foreword

Lance Ketchum has done it again! He has written another book that will be extremely useful for pastors, teachers, missionaries, evangelists, and all believers. In this book, he exhibits insightful exegesis of Scripture. His pastoral warmth shines through his writing. This book will be useful to overcome modern Gnosticism, syncretism, church-skipping, and dealing with the *Lukewarmite*. Each chapter builds upon the Rock, the Lord Jesus Christ, and His Word.

Dr. H.D. Williams

In addition, Dr. Ketchum explains the historical and cultural influences on the church at Colosse. He explains thoroughly the heretical teachings that influenced the Colossian Church. The questions at the end of every chapter are very helpful for guiding the student of Scripture. The questions will be extremely helpful for teachers in local churches, Bible schools, and seminaries, and for evoking thoughts for sermon preparation by pastors and evangelists.

Furthermore, this book explores the "doctrinal distinctiveness and practical distinctiveness" of the Lordship of Christ. This explanation of Colossians provides a comprehensive study of grace, *the* faith, salvation, saints, church, prayer, knowledge, wisdom, and spiritual understanding? It teaches sovereignty, redemption, forgiveness, the doctrine of Christ, reconciliation, and position and practice in Christ. The reader will learn about Christian service, various warnings about man's philosophies and traditions, angels, pragmatism, Zeitgeist, the old man, relationships, marriage, husbands and wives, children, and many other topics? All this and more is addressed in this complete and practical exegesis of the book of Colossians. This old sinner, saved by grace, hopes and prays this book will find its way into the library of every believer and church around the world.

H. D. Williams, M.D., Ph.D.
Cleveland, GA
2013

First Printing

February 2013

Studies in the Epistle to the Colossians

ISBN: 978-0-9860225-9-3

JESUS IS LORD?

List Price: **$13.95 each**
plus postage and handling

Additional copies can be obtained from:

Disciple Maker Ministries

**224 Fifth Avenue N.W.
Hutchinson, MN 55350**

(612) 750-5515

E-Mail: LanceKetchum@msn.com

Quantity prices are available.

TABLE OF CONTENTS

Jesus is Lord!

Studies in the Epistle to the Colossians

Introduction

THE LUKEWARMITES AND INCLUSIVISM

"[15] Love not the world, neither the things *that are* in the world. If any man love the world, the love of the Father is not in him. [16] For all that *is* in the world, the lust of the flesh, and the lust of the eyes, and the pride of life, is not of the Father, but is of the world. [17] And the world passeth away, and the lust thereof: but he that doeth the will of God abideth for ever. [18] Little children, it is the last time: and as ye have heard that antichrist shall come, even now are there many antichrists; whereby we know that it is the last time. [19] They went out from us, but they were not of us; for if they had been of us, they would *no doubt* have continued with us: but *they went out*, that they might be made manifest that they were not all of us. [20] But ye have an unction from the Holy One, and ye know all things. [21] I have not written unto you because ye know not the truth, but because ye know it, and that no lie is of the truth. [22] Who is a liar but he that denieth that Jesus is the Christ? He is antichrist, that denieth the Father and the Son. [23] Whosoever denieth the Son, the same hath not the Father: *(but) he that acknowledgeth the Son hath the Father also*" (I John 2:15-23).

It must seem strange to begin a study in the epistle to the Colossians in I John. Paul wrote the epistle to the Colossians during his first imprisonment at Rome. The primary subject matter of the epistle is to establish the eternal existence, pre-eminence and omnipotent Lordship of Jesus as the Son of God. The purpose of this epistle was to counteract a false teaching that had entered into early Christianity known as Gnosticism. Scofield's notes on Colossians 2:18 explain this heresy.

"The error against which Paul warned the Colossians later developed into the heresy called Gnosticism (from Gk. *gnosis*, meaning *knowledge*). This false teaching assigned

5

to Christ a place subordinate to the true Godhead, and undervalued the uniqueness and completeness of His redemptive work. It insisted that between a holy God and this earth a host of beings, angels, etc., formed a bridge, of which host was Christ was a member. This system included the worship of angels (v. 18) and a false asceticism (vv. 20-22). For all of these errors, the apostle had one remedy, a knowledge (*epignosis*; i.e. *full knowledge*, 1:8-10; 3:10) of the fullness of God in Jesus Christ. Paul is not afraid of wisdom, or knowledge, and refers to them frequently, but he does insist that the knowledge be according to divine revelation. His devastating answer to this false teaching is in 1:19 and 2:9, in which the Lord is revealed as the fullness of the Godhead bodily. The word "fullness" (Gr. *pleroma*) is the very word Gnosticism used for the entire host of intermediary beings between God and man. The incarnate Lord, crucified, risen, and ascended is the only Mediator between God and men (I Tim. 2:5)." (Scofield Reference Bible)

Although most of Christianity rejected Gnosticism and its devaluation of Jesus as just one of the many intermediaries between God and man, some did not reject the idea of *other* intermediaries. Many continued to view angels as intermediaries between God and man. Later, some misrepresented Mary, the mother of Jesus, as a mediator between God and man. Some taught that people could even pray with various dead *Saints,* who became intermediaries between God and man."

"Why did God Create Angels? The Creator Himself is so powerful and glorious that He cannot be approached in person by human beings. He alone 'hath immortality, dwelling in the light which no man can approach unto: whom no man hath seen, nor can see' (I Timothy 6:16). Angels do not have man's shortcomings, and can therefore act for God and represent Him when communicating with men and women. They bridge the huge gap between the holiness and perfection of God in heaven and the shortcomings of dying people on this planet."[1]

---

[1] Catholics Online, "Why did God Create Angels?", http://www.catholic.org/saints/angel.php#exist (accessed 2/11/2013).

"Do Catholics pray *to* saints? We pray with saints, not to them. . . Since saints led holy lives and are close to God in heaven, we feel that their prayers are particularly effective. Often we ask particular saints to pray for us if we feel they have a particular interest in our problem. For example, many people ask Saint Monica to pray for them if they have trouble with unanswered prayers, because Monica prayed for twenty years for her son to be converted. Finally her prayers were answered in a way she never dreamed of -- her son, Augustine, became a canonized saint and a Doctor of the Church."[2]

These heresies are serious because they actually deny the work of Christ in removing all mediators between God and man, but Himself. In the Old Covenant there was a Sacerdotal system of Prophets and Priests through which God spoke and through which He was approached. God did away with all of this in Jesus Christ. Any perversion of that reality is a both a direct attack upon the finished work of Jesus Christ. It is also a denial of the Lordship of Jesus Christ and His pre-eminence as the believer's Prophet, Priest, and King.

"For *there is* one God, and one mediator between God and men, the man Christ Jesus . . ." (I Timothy 2:5).

"[14] Seeing then that we have a great high priest, that is passed into the heavens, Jesus the Son of God, let us hold fast *our* profession. [15] For we have not an high priest which cannot be touched with the feeling of our infirmities; but was in all points tempted like as *we are, yet* without sin. [16] Let us therefore come boldly unto the throne of grace, that we may obtain mercy, and find grace to help in time of need" (Hebrews 4:14-16).

For centuries, the majority of Protestant and Baptist churches (true Baptists are not Protestants because they never were in Catholicism, and therefore they could not come out of Catholicism) rejected all forms of Gnosticism as heresy. True Bible believing Christians rejected the "traditions of men" in any form and held to the absolute

---

[2] Catholic Online, "Do Catholics Pray to Saints,"
www.catholic.org/saints/faq.php#pray (accessed 2/11/2013).

7

authority of the inspired Words of God to establish truth for life and practice. That absolute authority began to diminish under the onslaught of Theological Liberalism and its *birth child* New Evangelicalism, giving way to various degrees of Inclusivism.

If we believe we have the verbally inspired and inerrant Words of God in the sixty-six books of Scripture, then we must also believe we have an instruction book from God with absolute commands that are to be understood and obeyed absolutely. Anything less is unbelief.

> "But be ye doers of the word, and not hearers only, deceiving your own selves" (James 1:22).

When we do what God says in God's way, we are submitting to the Lordship of Christ. When we are disobedient to what God says, or when we co-operate with those we believe to be disobedient, we are denying the Lordship of Christ. Inclusivism proposes to include into the fellowship of a local church those individuals who hold beliefs that oppose those of that local church. Inclusivism proposes toleration of those holding to doctrines or practices contradicting biblical truth.

Many people leave independent, fundamental churches because independent, fundamental churches are not inclusive. They say they leave for many reasons. I have found there are **three basic reasons why people leave** independent, fundamental churches.

1. They believe the church is too strict *(therefore, they do not like the pastor).*
2. They disagree with what the church believes *(therefore, they do not like the pastor)*
3. They do not like the pastor.

We should measure the first two reasons according to the Word of God (I John 2:19). Many people leave (dis-fellowship) with a local church, because they believe it is too strict. *What does that mean?* That means that they have a practice of life that the pastor is preaching or teaching against that they are unwilling to relinquish. At

8

some time, they have come under conviction about that area of their life, have refused to recognize it as sin, have hardened their heart to the Lord, and are ready to run away from home. They usually do just that. What has happened? I John 2:19 has happened.

Others leave a local church (dis-fellowship) because they disagree with the doctrine (doctrinal distinctives) of that local church. This usually involves its teachings on the charismatic movement, Ecumenicism, or separation. These things are theological *hot potatoes* for people today. What has happened? I John 2:19 has just happened.

Even though these first two reasons for dis-fellowship are frequently stated by the words, "I don't like the pastor," there are some people who just don't like the pastor. Is hating someone ever a justifiable reason for doing anything? Of course, it is not. What is usually the real problem?

> "[11] For this is the message that ye heard from the beginning, that we should love one another. [12] Not as Cain, *who* was of that wicked one, and slew his brother. And wherefore slew he him? Because his own works were evil, and his brother's righteous" (I John 3:11-12).

Inclusivistic people often ask why separatist Christians will not include all other groups of Christians in their fellowship regardless of their doctrinal positions. They frequently make the statement, "After all they are good Christian people." What does it mean to be a *good Christian.* The word Christian signifies a person that is a follower of Christ. A *good Christian* must mean a person who excels at following the teachings of Jesus Christ. A few definitive questions need to be asked.

1. Can a person be a *good Christian* if he has not believed in the gospel of Jesus Christ? So we can exclude these from the realm of being *good Christians.*

2. Can a person be a *good Christian* if he refuses to be baptized by immersion? So we can exclude these from the realm of being *good Christians.*

9

3. Can a person be a *good Christian* if he practices fornication? How about social drinking? So we can exclude these from the realm of being *good Christians.*

4. Can a person be a *good Christian* if he refuses to be separate from apostasy? So we can exclude these from the realm of being *good Christians.*

5. Can a person be a *good Christian* if he does not tithe and give offerings? So we can exclude these from the realm of being *good Christians.*

6. Can a person be a *good Christian* if he is a member of a local church that holds to beliefs contrary to the Word of God? So we can exclude these from the realm of being *good Christians.*

7. To what degree can a person disagree with the Word of God and still consider himself a *good Christian*?

Most local church doctrinal statements define what that church expects of its members in beliefs, practices, and by how those perimeters define what is a *good Christian.* Some of these are very broad and inclusive. Others are very definitive and exclusive.

There are many reasons why a local church must be exclusive rather than inclusive. Although Christ invited everyone to follow Him, His grounds for following Him were exclusive.

> "He that is not with me is against me: and he that gathereth not with me scattereth" (Luke 11:23).

> "Then said Jesus unto his disciples, If any *man* will come after me, let him deny himself, and take up his cross, and follow me" (Matthew 16:24).

A local Church must be exclusive in order to establish doctrinal purity. There is only "one faith."

> "[16] All scripture *is* given by inspiration of God, and *is* profitable for doctrine, for reproof, for correction, for instruction in righteousness: [17] That the man of God may be perfect, throughly furnished unto all good works" (II Timothy 3:16-17).

"[4] *There is* one body, and one Spirit, even as ye are called in one hope of your calling; [5] One Lord, one faith, one baptism, [6] One God and Father of all, who *is* above all, and through all, and in you all" (Ephesians 4:4-6).

A local Church must be exclusive in order to maintain a pure gospel of grace and a common missional vision for that local church to remain in cooperative partnership with God (fellowship).

"[18] And Jesus came and spake unto them, saying, All power is given unto me in heaven and in earth. [19] Go ye therefore, and teach all nations, baptizing them in the name of the Father, and of the Son, and of the Holy Ghost: [20] Teaching them to observe all things whatsoever I have commanded you: and, lo, I am with you alway, *even* unto the end of the world. Amen" (Matthew 28:18-20).

"[6] I marvel that ye are so soon removed from him that called you into the grace of Christ unto another gospel: [7] Which is not another; but there be some that trouble you, and would pervert the gospel of Christ. [8] But though we, or an angel from heaven, preach any other gospel unto you than that which we have preached unto you, let him be accursed. [9] As we said before, so say I now again, If any *man* preach any other gospel unto you than that ye have received, let him be accursed. [10] For do I now persuade men, or God? or do I seek to please men? for if I yet pleased men, I should not be the servant of Christ. [11] But I certify you, brethren, that the gospel which was preached of me is not after man. [12] For I neither received it of man, neither was I taught *it*, but by the revelation of Jesus Christ" (Galatians 1:6-12).

When Joshua led Israel into the Promised Land, Ammonites, Moabites, Canaanites, Amalekites and many other assorted *"ites,"* surrounded the nation of Israel. However, the greatest threat to the security and safety of the Church of Christ are those from within our own ranks - the *Lukewarmites.* Christ sharply rebukes this type of professing believer in Revelation 3:14-19. They posed a great threat to the nation of Israel and this type of professing Christian poses an equal threat to local churches

The *Lukewarmites* are the Inclusivists of our day. They are *fence straddlers*. They practice a convenience theology. They hold to whatever beliefs that do not require them to take a stand, lose a friend, or for anyone to consider them *extreme*. They love people more than they love God. Be careful that you do not become a *Lukewarmite*.

Jesus is Lord!

Studies in the Epistle to the Colossians
Introduction
THE LUKEWARMITES AND INCLUSIVISM

1. What is the responsibility of a person who claims to believe in a verbally inspired and inerrant Word of God?

2. When we obey God's Word by doing what He says in the way He wants, to whom are we submitting?

3. Define *Inclusivist Policy*.

4. List the three basic reasons why people dis-fellowship with independent, fundamental churches.

5. What is the reality (real spiritual problem) behind each of these reasons?

6. In each of the above cases, what has happened according to I John 2:19?

7. Give seven things that would *exclude* someone from the realm of being a *good Christian*.

8. From the list above, do you think that you are exclusive or inclusive?

9. What is a *Lukewarmite* (see Revelation 3:14-19)?

10. Why is a *Lukewarmite* such a dangerous person in a local church?

Jesus is Lord!

Studies in the Epistle to the Colossians

Chapter One

WHEN IS JESUS LORD?

"[1] Paul, an apostle of Jesus Christ by the will of God, and Timotheus *our* brother, [2] To the saints and faithful brethren in Christ which are at Colosse: Grace *be* unto you, and peace, from God our Father and the Lord Jesus Christ. [3] We give thanks to God and the Father of our Lord Jesus Christ, praying always for you" (Colossians 1:1-3).

The phrase "Jesus is Lord" was the earliest and simplest confession of faith. When someone was asked for their doctrinal position, they could simply reply, Jesus is Lord. The testimony that Jesus is Lord is the *distinctive conviction* of the New Testament faith. However, what the phrase means has certainly lost its distinctiveness in today's world of relativism.

To the lost world of early Christianity, a Christian was distinguished as a person who had submitted to the authority of the words of a Nazarene peasant who was executed as a political criminal. These early Christians rejected all the philosophies of their day to live under the sovereign Lordship of Jesus as revealed to them by His Word.

It is important to understand the historical setting of the time of the writing of the Colossian Epistle. It was during the late part of the Greco-Roman period (approximately AD 60). The religious atmosphere was extensively *pluralistic*. There was enormous social pressure on the early Christians to become *pluralistic*.

The early church was under attack by the surrounding culture. As soon as any church became *pluralistic* in philosophy, the surrounding culture essentially absorbed it. That church then lost its distinctiveness as being truly Christian because it lost its testimony to the reality of the Lordship of Jesus. Even

14

though they continued proclaiming a testimony to the Lordship of Jesus, the reality of that testimony was a *sham.*

Four characteristics stand out as significant background for the letter to Colosse, establishing the religious scene of the day. We only need to read Acts 19:8-41 to note the similarities to our age. In this short text of church history, we find Jewish exorcists casting out demons. We find witchcraft and books of magic charms. We find pagan, licentious idolatry with the crafts and trades capitalizing on people's preoccupation with these things.

The area of Colosse was marked by a deeply *mystical atmosphere.*

They worshipped Artemis, the great *Mother Goddess.* This sexual cult emphasized human sexuality and body worship. There was a strong desire to tap into occult power much as the New Age movement today. They did this with drugs, astrology, sorcery, mysticism, and mediums. Presently, in our societies' great quest for pleasure through the satisfaction of desires and emotions, people often become involved in a number of variations of these things.

The religious life in Asia at this time was highly *syncretistic.*

At this period in history, *syncretism* involved the combination of three major religious systems:

1. Apostate Judaism
2. Christianity
3. The eastern occult mystery religions

The historical culmination of this *syncretism* was Roman Catholicism (by AD 300). We can only imagine the enormous sociological pressure this sort of atmosphere put upon anyone wanting to maintain a distinctively biblical position. This is much like the theological Inclusivism of modern times.

The epistle to the Colossians offers a simple solution to this *syncretis*m. The epistle to the Colossians demands *exclusive allegiance* to the Lordship of Jesus

Christ. It requires that the individual believer maintain his biblical distinctiveness and not allow the pressures of society to manipulate him into abandoning the purity of his allegiance to Jesus Christ.

The American society is a *melting pot* culture. The epistle to the Colossians presents similar pressures upon modern believers. Critical to the continuation of a biblical New Testament Christianity is the necessity to maintain a distinctively biblical belief system.

The Problem - any resistance to society's *syncretistic pressure* brought social ostracizing on those resisting and great conflict to the believer trying to maintain his distinctive New Testament beliefs.

Two dimensions of this conflict remain today:

1. The practice of biblical evangelism by the believer often brought rejection and criticism upon him from the dominant culture.
2. The believer had to deal with his inner temptations in desiring social acceptance in order to live according to the Word of God and to be approved of Him.

"[14] Of these things put *them* in remembrance, charging *them* before the Lord that they strive not about words to no profit, *but* to the subverting of the hearers. [15] Study to shew thyself approved unto God, a workman that needeth not to be ashamed, rightly dividing the word of truth. [16] But shun profane *and* vain babblings: for they will increase unto more ungodliness. [17] And their word will eat as doth a canker: of whom is Hymenaeus and Philetus; [18] Who concerning the truth have erred, saying that the resurrection is past already; and overthrow the faith of some. [19] Nevertheless the foundation of God standeth sure, having this seal, The Lord knoweth them that are his. And, Let every one that nameth the name of Christ depart from iniquity. [20] But in a great house there are not only vessels of gold and of silver, but also of wood and of earth; and some to honour, and some to dishonour. [21] If a man therefore purge himself from these, he shall be a vessel unto honour, sanctified, and meet for the master's use, *and* prepared unto every good work" (II Timothy 2:15-21).

This biblical test proves if Jesus really is Lord of a believer's life. It would also be the test to see if that believer's faith sees beyond the temporal existence of this life.

In order for the believer to stand against the social pressure to compromise his distinctive New Covenant beliefs, he needed to focus upon the power of God in the indwelling Holy Spirit. The proper response to the social pressure of a *syncretistic society* is the exaltation of Jesus Christ as Lord in every practice of life, regardless of the cost to the believer personally.

Living faith puts the will of the Lord first in every decision. Christians need to intellectually understand, accept, voluntarily act upon, and reverently submit to the Lordship of Christ. They represent this submission with a biblical and separated lifestyle. If not, a testimony to the Lordship of Christ is a *sham*.

The Colossian Epistle is a *warning* and *instruction* about a necessary response to danger from the pressure of *syncretism*. The Colossian Epistle establishes the necessity of a pre-eminent relationship in submission to the revealed will of Jesus Christ and His full sufficiency as our personal representative. The heart of the epistle is the heart of the Gospel. We are complete in Christ (Colossians 2:9-10, paraphrase of 2:9: "For in Jesus the divine essence of the Godhead has taken permanent residence in a body of humanity").

Jesus has identified Himself with humanity for all eternity by becoming human. He will continue as a glorified human (God united with humanity) throughout eternity. Since the Son of God is willing to make this sacrifice for us, it seems a "reasonable service" that we should be willing to make any necessary sacrifice to maintain our distinct identity with Him as Lord.

The resolution of a genuine believer proclaiming Jesus to be his Lord must be a resolution that holds exclusively to the Word of Jesus. Such a person must resist all pressure toward syncretism and compromise. Although this may be viewed as narrow-minded prejudice towards other *socially accepted* religious beliefs, the truths of John

17

14:6 and Acts 4:12 still reflect the mind of Christ in the matter. If Jesus truly is Lord in one's life, what the Lord says about these issues will take preeminence over public opinion or social pressures to compromise.

> "Jesus saith unto him, I am the way, the truth, and the life: no man cometh unto the Father, but by me" (John 14:6).

> "Neither is there salvation in any other: for there is none other name under heaven given among men, whereby we must be saved" (Acts 4:12).

Central to the testimony that Jesus is Lord is the willingness to maintain a distinctive identity with the "narrow way" Gospel of Jesus Christ. Any movement away from that Gospel is a step away from the Lordship of Christ. It is also a step away from identifying with His sacrifice for our sin. If we abandon the "narrow way" Gospel of Christ, we also abandon the Lordship of Christ in our lives and contradict our testimony to His Lordship (see Colossians 1:23).

> "And why call ye me, Lord, Lord, and do not the things which I say" (Luke 6:46)?

> "[13] Ye call me Master and Lord: and ye say well; for *so* I am. [14] If I then, *your* Lord and Master, have washed your feet; ye also ought to wash one another's feet. [15] For I have given you an example, that ye should do as I have done to you. [16] Verily, verily, I say unto you, The servant is not greater than his lord; neither he that is sent greater than he that sent him. [17] If ye know these things, happy are ye if ye do them" (John 13:13-17).

A believer manifests the reality of a true testimony to the Lordship of Jesus when tries to live what Jesus taught. We will fail often. We will fall frequently, but we will continue in the effort with every ounce of our being. That is when Jesus is Lord!

Jesus is Lord!

Studies in the Epistle to the Colossians
Chapter One
WHEN IS JESUS LORD?

1. What was the earliest and simplest confession of faith?
   A. What did that testimony mean?
   B. What does that testimony mean to *you* (personally)?

2. What were the historical and cultural influences on the believers at the time of the writing of the Epistle of Colossians?
   A. Do you think the same types of influence effect believers today?
   B. If so, how is the truth of this epistle beneficial for our time?

3. Define the four given characteristic influences on the believer at the time of the writing of the Colossians Epistle.

4. What is *syncretism*?

5. Why is the heart of the epistle the heart of the Gospel?

6. Paraphrase Colossians 2:9 and explain what it means.

7. What decision(s) do you think you need to make about these truths?

Jesus is Lord!

Studies in the Epistle to the Colossians
Chapter Two
THE STRUGGLE IN OUR RESPONSIBILITY TO THE LORDSHIP OF CHRIST

"[1] Paul, an apostle of Jesus Christ by the will of God, and Timotheus *our* brother, [2] To the saints and faithful brethren in Christ which are at Colosse: Grace *be* unto you, and peace, from God our Father and the Lord Jesus Christ. [3] We give thanks to God and the Father of our Lord Jesus Christ, praying always for you, [4] Since we heard of your faith in Christ Jesus, and of the love *which ye have* to all the saints, [5] For the hope which is laid up for you in heaven, whereof ye heard before in the word of the truth of the gospel; [6] Which is come unto you, as *it is* in all the world; and bringeth forth fruit, as *it doth* also in you, since the day ye heard *of it*, and knew the grace of God in truth: [7] As ye also learned of Epaphras our dear fellowservant, who is for you a faithful minister of Christ; [8] Who also declared unto us your love in the Spirit" (Colossians 1:1-8).

Problems in local churches are nothing new. We might even go as far as to say these problems are a historical constant - things that happen constantly throughout history. The great struggle of "the faith" and "for the faith" is twofold. These two struggles are both pastoral and parental. Pastors struggle with congregations in these two areas and parents struggle with their children in these two areas.

1. There is the struggle to get people to know the truth and accept the truth - to believe it.
2. There is the struggle to get people to live and obey the truth they profess to know and believe.

The first thing we want to establish about the epistle to Colosse is that it comes with the authority of God's inspiration (Colossians 1:1).

The Bible came from God, not men. The Bible is an instruction book for living. Central to the epistle's purpose is to warn believers about false teachings that might lead them away from their submission to the Lordship of Christ. Once led astray, their focus of their ministry is perverted from others onto themselves.

In verse one, when Paul says he is an "Apostle of the Lord," he is proclaiming his authority to speak for God. He is a voice of God to the people. He is expecting opposition to what he is going to say. "I Paul am made a minister . . ." (1:23).

Paul understood that the work he was doing was a response to a *divine directive*. He could not do anything else and remain in the will of God (see v. 1, "by the will of God"). The fact that Paul was an Apostle was the criterion that gave absolute authority to the words He wrote and spoke. In order to refute what Paul said, those who disagreed with him had to question his calling. In doing so, they questioned the credibility of what he said.

The second thing that needs to be established is that Paul addresses the letter to the "saints and faithful brethren in Christ which are at Colosse." The word "saints" is from the Greek word *hagios* (hag'-ee-os). It does not imply moral excellence. It signifies a distinctive people set apart from the world through regeneration and unto the work of Christ. The word refers to a people who have benefited positionally by accepting and confessing Jesus as their Lord. "Saints" is a word that describes our position and our *identity* as believer/priests before God.

In doing so, they recognized themselves as having been redeemed by Jesus Christ and therefore, distinctively belonging to God. They also recognized they had been set apart from the world to serve Him through ministry to others. "Saints" is a word that describes a position of *responsibility*.

"[19] What? know ye not that your body is the temple of the Holy Ghost *which is* in you, which ye have of God, and ye are not your own? [20] For ye are bought with a price:

therefore glorify God in your body, and in your spirit, which are God's" (I Corinthians 6:19-20).

"²² For he that is called in the Lord, *being* a servant, is the Lord's freeman: likewise also he that is called, *being* free, is Christ's servant. ²³ Ye are bought with a price; be not ye the servants of men" (I Corinthians. 7:22-23).

The word "faithful" is from the Greek word *pistos* (pis-tos'). "Faithful" describes the way in which a believer maintains his identity with Christ and fulfills his responsibilities in service as a believer/priest. The use of the word "faithful" to describe believers means they could be relied upon to do what the Word of God directed them to do. Loyalty to Christ's Lordship was their highest priority.

The words "at Colosse" tell us this was an epistle written to a local church. Although this may seem insignificant, the implications are very broad. It is difficult (if not impossible) to remain distinctively biblical without a support group to re-enforce those distinctives. A large aspect of the purpose of the local church is personal accountability to a peer group (*positive re-enforcement*). Therefore, God established an organization to *polarize* and *reinforce* the corporate values of that organization (the local church). Read I Kings 19:4-21 for a negative comparative example.

"⁴ But he himself went a day's journey into the wilderness, and came and sat down under a juniper tree: and he requested for himself that he might die; and said, It is enough; now, O LORD, take away my life; for I *am* not better than my fathers. ⁵ And as he lay and slept under a juniper tree, behold, then an angel touched him, and said unto him, Arise *and* eat. ⁶ And he looked, and, behold, *there was* a cake baken on the coals, and a cruse of water at his head. And he did eat and drink, and laid him down again. ⁷ And the angel of the LORD came again the second time, and touched him, and said, Arise *and* eat; because the journey *is* too great for thee. ⁸ And he arose, and did eat and drink, and went in the strength of that meat forty days and forty nights unto Horeb the mount of God. ⁹ And he came thither unto a cave, and lodged there; and, behold, the word of the LORD *came* to him, and he said unto him, What

22

doest thou here, Elijah? [10] And he said, I have been very jealous for the LORD God of hosts: for the children of Israel have forsaken thy covenant, thrown down thine altars, and slain thy prophets with the sword; and I, *even* I only, am left; and they seek my life, to take it away. [11] And he said, Go forth, and stand upon the mount before the LORD. And, behold, the LORD passed by, and a great and strong wind rent the mountains, and brake in pieces the rocks before the LORD; *but* the LORD *was* not in the wind: and after the wind an earthquake; *but* the LORD *was* not in the earthquake: [12] And after the earthquake a fire; *but* the LORD *was* not in the fire: and after the fire a still small voice. [13] And it was *so*, when Elijah heard *it*, that he wrapped his face in his mantle, and went out, and stood in the entering in of the cave. And, behold, *there came* a voice unto him, and said, What doest thou here, Elijah? [14] And he said, I have been very jealous for the LORD God of hosts: because the children of Israel have forsaken thy covenant, thrown down thine altars, and slain thy prophets with the sword; and I, *even* I only, am left; and they seek my life, to take it away. [15] And the LORD said unto him, Go, return on thy way to the wilderness of Damascus: and when thou comest, anoint Hazael *to be* king over Syria: [16] And Jehu the son of Nimshi shalt thou anoint *to be* king over Israel: and Elisha the son of Shaphat of Abelmeholah shalt thou anoint *to be* prophet in thy room. [17] And it shall come to pass, *that* him that escapeth the sword of Hazael shall Jehu slay: and him that escapeth from the sword of Jehu shall Elisha slay. [18] Yet I have left *me* seven thousand in Israel, all the knees which have not bowed unto Baal, and every mouth which hath not kissed him. [19] So he departed thence, and found Elisha the son of Shaphat, who *was* plowing *with* twelve yoke *of oxen* before him, and he with the twelfth: and Elijah passed by him, and cast his mantle upon him. [20] And he left the oxen, and ran after Elijah, and said, Let me, I pray thee, kiss my father and my mother, and *then* I will follow thee. And he said unto him, Go back again: for what have I done to thee? [21] And he returned back from him, and took a yoke of oxen, and slew them, and boiled their flesh with the instruments of the oxen, and gave unto the people, and they did eat. Then he arose, and went after Elijah, and ministered unto him" (I Kings 19:4-21).

According to verse four, Elijah was defeated, discouraged, and all alone. The words "it is enough" essentially say, "I have had enough. I quit." According to verses ten and fourteen, Elijah believed that no one would stand with him in opposing evil and promoting truth. In verse eighteen, God revealed to him that he was a single part of a larger whole. He was part of a collective and distinctive group of believers with the same identity and purpose, experiencing similar trials and temptations. In verses 19-21 God gives him a partner (Elisha).

The third thing we want to see is that there was a sense of *mutual obligation* between believers (Colossians 1:3). They prayed for one another. They were not in competition with one another. There was a sense of family among this congregation of "saints."

Paul was thankful "to God" for their faithfulness. Christians should pray for one another and for other local churches to be faithful. When any local church fails in its faithfulness to the Lord, that unfaithfulness brings reproach upon the Lord and all other local churches. When any local church falters or fails, it reflects on all believers.

Paul's prayer was *intercessory*. He met with God and spoke with Him on the behalf of this local church. According to verse four, Paul had been praying for them since these people first believed and formed the local church at Colosse. Paul prayed for them even though he was not a member or even knew any of the members personally (other than their pastor, Epaphras). Therefore, praying for the success of other local churches was a habitual and regular part of Paul's prayer life.

The substance of Paul's prayer for this local church shows his intent to provide theological reinforcement for their continued distinctiveness and faithfulness to the Gospel message. According to verses 5-6, the Gospel provides *solidarity* for fellowship between local churches. It is the central focal point for the basis of any real fellowship. The erosion and distortion of the truth of the Gospel message has historically destroyed fellowship between local churches. No local church can be said to be faithful to the Lordship of Jesus Christ that is unfaithful to the propagation of His Gospel of salvation by grace (alone) though faith (alone) in Christ (alone). As we will see later, this epistle carries warnings against certain perversions of the Gospel of grace (2:8-23).

The fourth thing we want to emphasize is that when a pure Gospel of grace ("grace of God in truth") is *maintained* in its purity, it will advance and bring forth fruit (Colossians 1:6). God substantiated this principal evidentially in the local church at Colosse. The Gospel of grace continued to bring forth fruit. Only the Gospel of grace detailing the finished work of Christ is the Gospel that "bringeth forth fruit."

The true Gospel that "bringeth forth fruit" *must be understood* from the perspective of the "grace of God in truth." When the truth (the details of what Christ has accomplished in His death, burial, and resurrection) is taken out of the Gospel (or perverted), the power of the Gospel to save is removed because it is no longer the Gospel (Galatians 1: 6-7, "which is not another").

Paul was writing this epistle to support what their pastor (Epaphras) was trying to teach them and about what he was warning them (Colossians 1:7-8). Paul calls Epaphras his "dear fellowservant" (co-laborer in the Gospel). Paul joins himself with Epaphras and identifies himself with Epaphras' ministry to establish these people in biblical truth. Someone was undermining the foundation of that truth by perverting the Gospel.

In Paul's support of Epaphras, he re-enforces the authority of Epaphras. The stability of future generations of believers in this church would depend upon them following the spiritual leadership of Epaphras as he taught truth. From that perspective, read I Corinthians 3:9-11.

"[9] For we are labourers together with God: ye are God's husbandry, *ye are* God's building. [10] According to the grace of God which is given unto me, as a wise masterbuilder, I have laid the foundation, and another buildeth thereon. But let every man take heed how he buildeth thereupon. [11] For other foundation can no man lay than that is laid, which is Jesus Christ" (I Corinthians 3:9-11).

Stonemasons built upon a foundation to construct a building. The foundation was the most critical part of a building of stones. It needed to be sturdy, level, true, and laid upon solid ground. I Corinthians 3:9-11 is a metaphor referring to the building of a local church. The layers of stones are different generations of believers. Local church leadership must stabilize and ground each generation in the same truths (anchored upon the foundation) before there can be stability for the next generation of believers. The danger is that each generation will be tempted to compromise to some degree, creating instability in the succeeding generations depending on the degree of their compromise.

Paul calls Epaphras a "faithful minister." He was loyal and faithful to the established truths of God's Word and to the Gospel of grace. He faithfully preached these truths. He was committed to teaching truth regardless of what it cost him personally. He refused to compromise the truth of the Gospel of grace to make it culturally acceptable.

Epaphras was a *seed planter*. He knew if he sowed perverted and corrupted seed of truth in someone's life, he would reap a perverted and corrupted life. Any *seed planter* knows the *surety* of the crop he harvests is dependent upon the *surety* of the seed he sows. Do not be upset with a *seed planter* if he disagrees with you over what you think is a minor point of doctrine. Instead, *listen carefully*. He just may be trying to make sure of the *seed* he is planting.

Jesus is Lord!

Studies in the Epistle to the Colossians
Chapter Two
THE STRUGGLE IN OUR RESPONSIBILITY TO THE LORDSHIP OF CHRIST

1. Why is it important for the Apostle Paul to establish that the epistle to Colosse comes with the authority of God?

2. What are two reasons why Paul states he is an "Apostle of the Lord"?

3. What does the word "saints" imply about the people it describes?

4. What does the word "faithful" describe about the above two things?

5. Discuss the significance of the words "at Colosse."

6. Read I Kings 19:4-21. How is this portion of Scripture an example of the problem that might result when believers ignore the things discussed in the previous question and how did God help Elijah in his defeated spirit?

7. Read Colossians 1:3. What was going on that shows a sense of mutual obligation between believers?

8. Read Colossians 1:5-6. What was the central focal point that provided solidarity for fellowship between local churches?

9. When a pure gospel of grace is maintained in purity of truth, what will be the result according to Colossians 1:6?

10. According to Colossians 1:7-8, for who was Paul seeking support and what was he seeking to support in the writing of this epistle?

11. Discuss the *building* metaphor of I Corinthians 3:9-11 that exemplifies this struggle.

12. Epaphras was a SEED PLANTER. Why should believers not get upset when a seed planter labors over what seems to be a minor point of doctrine?

Jesus is Lord!

Studies in the Epistle to the Colossians
Chapter Three
THE SPECIFICS AND OBJECTIVES OF PRAYER

A new Christian is very susceptible to being led astray into false doctrines and false practices. Most new Christians have little or no discernment in doctrinal issues because they have never been discipled in the Word of God. Often, they do not understand the importance of being discipled. They make little effort to learn God's Word because they do not understand the dangers of false teachers and false teaching. They do not faithfully attend Sunday school classes and preaching services. They are like new born infants needing constant care and bottle feeding. They do not know how to study the Bible and consider the Bible to be a book they cannot understand. We must begin their discipleship by explaining all of these various things to them. We have to explain the dangers to which they will be exposed. We must keep new Christians in prayer. New Christians that are not thoroughly discipled the first year seldom remain faithful into a second year. They will be deceived and drawn away into corrupt churches or worldliness.

"⁹ For this cause we also, since the day we heard *it*, do not cease to pray for you, and to desire that ye might be filled with the knowledge of his will in all wisdom and spiritual understanding; ¹⁰ That ye might walk worthy of the Lord unto all pleasing, being fruitful in every good work, and increasing in the knowledge of God; ¹¹ Strengthened with all might, according to his glorious power, unto all patience and longsuffering with joyfulness; ¹² Giving thanks unto the Father, which hath made us meet to be partakers of the inheritance of the saints in light: ¹³ Who hath delivered us from the power of darkness, and hath translated *us* into the kingdom of his dear Son:" (Colossians 1:9-13).

Prayer is the necessary discipline for discernment.

"For this cause" society confronts and bombards Christians everywhere and every day with questions of life and practice. These questions require careful consideration. Most of the time there is no opportunity to make careful consideration before people make decisions. Believers in a local church must learn to pray for one another about decisions they must make each day. Paul prayed for the believers at Colosse regularly. Paul prayed for *two specifics*:

1. Paul prayed for their discernment of the will of God (vs. 9-10).
2. Paul prayed for God's enabling power so that they might perform God's will (v. 11).

This regular prayer was prompted by the good report detailed in verses 4-8. There is a natural incentive to pray for faithful people based upon understanding that God will bless the efforts of faithful people in ministry.

The Specifics of Prayer

The word "desire" in Colossians 1:9 is from the Greek word *aiteo* (ahee-teh'-o). In this context, it is a specific word for prayer that signifies *to ask* for something to be *given*, not *done*. In this context, it refers to the *illumination* of the truth of God's Word. God reveals His will through His Word. God will not *illuminate* His truth until we are *committed to a course of action that involves us in that truth*.

"If any man will do his will, he shall know of the doctrine, whether it be of God, or *whether* I speak of myself" (John 7:17).

Paul prays that these believers at Colosse might have *knowledge*. *Knowledge* is from the Greek word *epignosis* (ep-ig'-no-sis) and refers to *perfect* or *mature knowledge*. This is a *knowledge* that fully grasps and penetrates a subject. This *knowledge* involves *intimate details* and *familiarity*. This is the *knowledge* that is necessary for discernment.

The *knowledge* to which Paul refers is directly opposed to the *knowledge* worship of Gnosticism. The *knowledge* to which Paul refers comes solely from God's *illumination* of inspired Scriptures through study and pastoral instruction. The kind of *knowledge* to which Paul refers is purely *Bible sourced*. This kind of *knowledge* comes from studying the Word of God and "rightly dividing the word of truth" (II Timothy 2:15).

Gnosticism believes salvation comes through achieving the highest level of *knowledge* (*saving knowledge*). This corrupting influence of early Gnosticism was corrupting the Gospel. Gnostic salvation came to the *initiate* as he progressed through *Twelve Dominions of Light* (*knowledge*). A person *achieved* salvation once he ascended to the twelfth level of this knowledge. These twelve levels of knowledge are listed in the book *Gnosis On The Silk Road* by Hans-Joachim Klimkeit. These twelve levels of knowledge help us understand what Paul was dealing with and why these early Christians needed spiritual discernment about integrating these false concepts into Christianity. They are:

1. Father of Light – dominion
2. The Mother of Life – wisdom
3. The First Man (Ohrmizd) – "victory," salvation
4. The five sons of the First Man – contentment, joy
5. The Friend of Light – zeal
6. The Great Builder – truth
7. The Living Spirit – faith
8. The Third Messenger – patience
9. The Column of Glory – righteousness
10. Jesus the Splendor – kindness
11. The Maiden of Light – harmony, mildness
12. Vahman, the Great Nous – Light[3]

---

[3] Klimkeit, Hans-Joachim, Translation and presentation. *Gnosis on the Silk Road: Gnostic Texts from Central Asia* (New York, NY: HarperCollins Publishers, 1993), pages 77-78.

These twelve progressions toward *complete* knowledge (see Paul's statement in Colossians 2:10) are what New Age people call *self-actualization*. Once a person achieved this final state of *knowledge,* it was believed that he actually became part of the *Great Nous* (Light). It is easy to see how easily this could be integrated into a *Christianity* that was not purely *Bible sourced* in doctrine. It is also easy to see how many Christians, saved out of the pagan religions, could be so easily led astray into this integrationism (syncretism). In this heresy, salvation became a quest for *knowledge* (Light).

In ancient Babylonia, the religion of Gnosticism was manifested in the Towers (Ziggurats) of Babylon. These kinds of towers are found all over the world in many pagan cultures. They consisted of towers (pyramids or mounds) made up of stones, bricks, or earth amassed in various numbers of levels. The various levels were accessed by steps or ramps. The highest level (the *summit*) was where the idol was erected and where sacrifices were offered. Only certain individuals were allowed on the summit level (usually a High Priest and royal rulers who were believed to be the descendants of the god –the idea of *royal blood* comes from this).

In Babylonian Gnosticism, the Towers represented the *journey to enlightenment.* The various levels represented the intermediaries of a pantheon of gods. The supreme god of the pantheon was *Allah.* The Moon god was represented by the Crescent. He was married to the Sun-goddess. All the stars were believed to be their offspring. Therefore, *Allah* is not the Arabic name for the God of the Bible.

A highly complex and secretive set of religious rites evolved in the Babylonian cults. Disciples advanced by going through a succession of *secret initiations* into higher and higher levels of knowledge (*gnosis*) of the mysteries of the cosmos; until they professed they had obtained *god-like powers*. These various levels represent the various phases of the moon (eight phases: new moon, waxing crescent, first quarter, waxing gibbous, full moon, waning gibbous, last quarter, and waning crescent). The moon completes these eight phases every twenty-nine days, twelve hours and forty-four plus minutes. The Jews added a month (Adar II) every nineteen years to compensate so as to correspond with the solar calendar.

The practices of Gnosticism and moon worship can be traced back to ancient Nimrod.

> "[8] And Cush {*son of Noah's son Ham*} begat Nimrod: he began to be a mighty one in the earth. [9] He was a mighty hunter before the LORD: wherefore it is said, Even as Nimrod the mighty hunter before the LORD. [10] And the beginning of his kingdom was Babel, and Erech, and Accad, and Calneh, in the land of Shinar" (Genesis 10:8-10).

Knowledge of God's Word must never end with mere intellectual awareness. The truth of God's Word must fill our minds and overflow into a lifestyle that corresponds with the moral aspect of God's will for the conduct of our lives. This *perfect or mature knowledge* is divided into two categories both coming by illumination.

1. *Wisdom* - this is a general overall knowledge of God's Word in an applicational sense.

2. *Spiritual understanding* - this is a specific ability given to the believer to grasp the Spirit of God's insight. This insight then *discerns* between the false and the true.

The cultural pressure on believers to become syncretistic (meaning they began to accept varying beliefs contrary to the truth of God's Word) was enormous. Syncretism is the merging or blending of all forms of religious beliefs. This practice of integrating pagan religious beliefs with biblical truth continues to be practiced today.

Paul prays for the believers at Colosse to receive "wisdom" and "spiritual understanding." These two necessities for discernment are received *from* God *by* illumination. These two necessities are the only means through which they would be able to maintain the distinctive *Bible based* beliefs to which that they presently held. Without "wisdom" and "spiritual understanding" they would be quickly absorbed into their syncretistic society.

First Objective of Prayer – "walk worthy of the Lord"

Discerning knowledge is a perfect or mature knowledge of God's will in the areas of wisdom and understanding. This discerning knowledge results in a "walk worthy of the Lord" (v. 10). "Walk" refers to a specific order of behavior. "Worthy" refers to something that carries the same influence as another thing. The objective for believers in having "all wisdom and spiritual understanding" was that their lives would be conducted in such a way as to carry the *same influence upon people as the Lord Jesus.*

"Wisdom and understanding" are of little value if they do not result in the same *action* or *practice* as the Lord. Knowledge meant much more than acquiring a certain level of spiritual understanding. Knowledge was only a reality if the spiritual understanding was translated into living ("walk"). This "walk" is according to knowledge when it is "pleasing to God in every way."

Perfect or discerning knowledge of the will of God, in the areas of "wisdom and understanding," will also be manifested by the believer bearing fruit "in every good work." The KJV translation is somewhat misleading. It should read, "constantly bearing fruit as a result of pleasing God in every good work and increasing *by means* of the perfect and thorough knowledge of God."

The objective of Paul's prayer was not that these believers increase in knowledge, but that they would be *constantly bearing fruit and increasing in numbers* as a result of having all "wisdom and spiritual understanding."

Second Objective of Prayer – "Strengthened with all might"

Being "strengthened with all might" is still another objective of having "all wisdom and spiritual understanding" or discernment. The idea is that through this "wisdom and spiritual understanding" believers would receive the strengthening ability that would enable them to do that which was right in God's eyes. The implication is that there is *intrinsic spiritual power* in "wisdom and spiritual understanding."

"Glory" is a reference to the bright light over the mercy seat. It was a physical manifestation of the *power of the holiness of God.* When the believer lives his life according to the perfect knowledge of God's Word, that believer will be "glorifying" God. He will manifest the power of the goodness, holiness, and righteousness of God to the world. The "light" that is God is not in the knowledge or truth about God, but in the *living, actualization* of those truths. The believer that lives these truths does not become God. He merely accurately reveals who God is by restoring the image of God in his life. This is what it means to bring God glory.

> "[13] Ye are the salt of the earth: but if the salt have lost his savour, wherewith shall it be salted? it is thenceforth good for nothing, but to be cast out, and to be trodden under foot of men. [14] Ye are the light of the world. A city that is set on an hill cannot be hid. [15] Neither do men light a candle, and put it under a bushel, but on a candlestick; and it giveth light unto all that are in the house. [16] Let your light so shine before men, that they may see your good works, and glorify your Father which is in heaven" (Matthew 5:13-16).

Somehow, Christianity has come to suffer under the misnomer that the Holy of Holies is a place where we visit occasionally rather than the place where we live. Every believer is "mercy seated" (*propitiated* - Romans 3:25). However, it is only the believer with a perfect (living) knowledge of God's Word who is able to manifest the power of God's goodness, holiness, and righteousness. God's goodness, holiness, and righteousness cannot be understood apart from the revelation of His Word. A source of our highest strength lies in the *practical translation* of the goodness, holiness, and righteousness of God. This *practical translation* is revealed through His Word in our everyday lives - living the goodness, holiness, and righteousness of God.

The Third Objective of Prayer – "Unto all patience and longsuffering with joyfulness"

The living of God's goodness, holiness, and righteousness in our lives will result in *patience* and *longsuffering*. In the Gnostic mindset, this could not be achieved until the eighth level of knowledge and after years and years of pursuit. Paul says it is immediately available to the believer willing to yield his will to God's will.

"Patience" is the long holding out of the mind before it gives room to action. "Patience" here is forbearing involving our relationships with people. A Christian who has to deal with a person who is antagonistic toward him or God's Word can be said to have "patience" if he does not allow that individual to provoke him or cause him to blaze up in anger.

"Longsuffering" is forbearing involving things. The person who is "longsuffering" is the individual who, under trials or difficulties of life, is not discouraged by them.

Neither of these is a mere endurance or a toleration of something for a period of time. "Longsuffering" is daily courageously contending with the hindrances of life. "Longsuffering" is daily courageously contending with the persecutions and the temptations that confront the believer. "Longsuffering" is daily courageously contending with the issues of life in what he believes inwardly and what attacks and confronts those beliefs outwardly. "Patience" and "longsuffering" do not allow the many times we fail to defeat us. "Patience" and "longsuffering" means we continue on even after we have been knocked down many times.

The Value of Living God's Goodness, Holiness, and Righteousness

"Patience and longsuffering," when seen only as a need to endure a wrong or injustice, will result in nothing but a sour and bitter disposition. When we understand God's purposes behind "patience and longsuffering" and the potential blessings of God in our lives, "patience and longsuffering," will be accompanied by "joyfulness."

The Fourth Objective of Prayer - "Giving thanks unto the Father, who has made us fit" (v.12)

Constant thanksgiving should be given to the Father because of the standing the believer has "in Christ." To be "made meet" (or *made fit*) means to make a person sufficient, ready, and prepared. Through the finished work of Christ, the individual who puts faith in Christ is "rendered fit," or is *pre-qualified* by the work of Christ. Christ has presently made us "participators with Him" in his inheritance in the realm of His light. The believer does not need to wait until he has achieved the final *twelfth stage* of *enlightenment*. The Christian's life begins with the believer living in the realm of God's "light." We build from that beginning. Peter explains this in detail in his answer to Gnosticism's heresies.

> "[1] Simon Peter, a servant and an apostle of Jesus Christ, to them that have obtained like precious faith with us through the righteousness of God and our Saviour Jesus Christ: [2] Grace and peace be multiplied unto you through the knowledge of God, and of Jesus our Lord, [3] According as his divine power hath given unto us all things that *pertain* unto life and godliness, through the knowledge of him that hath called us to glory and virtue: [4] Whereby are given unto us exceeding great and precious promises: that by these ye might be partakers of the divine nature, having escaped the corruption that is in the world through lust. [5] And beside this, giving all diligence, add to your faith virtue; and to virtue knowledge; [6] And to knowledge temperance; and to temperance patience; and to patience godliness; [7] And to godliness brotherly kindness; and to brotherly kindness charity. [8] For if these things be in you, and abound, they make *you that ye shall* neither *be* barren nor unfruitful in the knowledge of our Lord Jesus Christ" (II Peter 1:1-8).

The list of spiritual qualities in II Peter 1:5-8, that the believer is admonished to add to this *new beginning*, is for the purpose of validating the reality of that *new beginning.* The truth of God's Word is a kingdom of itself. Validating that we live in that realm of "light" is done by living the "light" and by our becoming "light."

"[1] Therefore being justified by faith, we have peace with God through our Lord Jesus Christ: [2] By whom also <u>we have access by faith into this grace wherein we stand,</u> and rejoice in hope of the glory of God. [3] And not only *so*, but we glory in tribulations also: knowing that tribulation worketh patience; [4] And patience, experience; and experience, hope: [5] And hope maketh not ashamed; because the love of God is shed abroad in our hearts by the Holy Ghost which is given unto us" (Romans 5:1-5).

We have been made qualified to function and live in the *Kingdom of Truth* (v. 13) the moment we trust in the finished work of Christ. We have been delivered out from the tyranny of disorder and the confusion of this world of Satan. We have been translated, or transferred, to a well ordered sovereignty of enabling "grace," with its boundaries established by the truth of God's Word. We live within that sovereignty when we yield to the indwelling Holy Spirit and are supernaturally enabled to live the truths of God's Word. The sovereignty of the kingdom exists wherever we live and exist. We take it with us wherever we go. Jesus is always Lord of the *Kingdom of His Grace.*

Jesus is Lord!

Studies in the Epistle to the Colossians
Chapter Three
THE SPECIFICS AND OBJECTIVES OF PRAYER

1. Read Colossians 1:9-11. For what two specifics did Paul pray in the lives of the believers at Colosse?

2. According to verses 4-8, what was Paul's natural incentive to pray for this local church? How do you view your investment of time in prayer?

3. "Desire" (v. 9) is a specific word for prayer that signifies "to _ _ _ for something to be _ _ _ _ _, not done."

4. According to John 7:17, what is the requirement before God will reveal His will through His Word to an individual?

5. The Greek word translated "knowledge" in verse 9 is *epignosis*. Does this refer to merely an intellectual knowledge of something or someone? If not, explain what this means.

6. What would happen to these believers and this local church without "wisdom" and "spiritual understanding"?
    A. Define "wisdom"?
    B. Define "spiritual understanding"?

7. Verse 10 refers to Paul's objective in praying for these believers. What two results will the *perfect knowledge* of God's will bring about in the areas of wisdom and understanding?

8. What is Paul's second objective of prayer in verse 11?

9. The word "glory" is a reference to the bright light over the mercy seat. Of what was it a physical manifestation?

10. What was Paul's third objective of prayer from verse 11?

11. What was Paul's fourth objective of prayer from verse 12?

12. Where has the believer been made qualified to function and live by the finished work of Jesus Christ?

Jesus is Lord!

Studies in the Epistle to the Colossians

Chapter Four

THE SOVEREIGNTY OF JESUS IN HIS PRESENT KINGDOM OF LIGHT

"[12] Giving thanks unto the Father, which hath made us meet to be partakers of the inheritance of the saints in light: [13] Who hath delivered us from the power of darkness, and hath translated *us* into the kingdom of his dear Son: [14] In whom we have redemption through his blood, *even* the forgiveness of sins: [15] Who is the image of the invisible God, the firstborn of every creature: [16] For by him were all things created, that are in heaven, and that are in earth, visible and invisible, whether *they be* thrones, or dominions, or principalities, or powers: all things were created by him, and for him: [17] And he is before all things, and by him all things consist. [18] And he is the head of the body, the church: who is the beginning, the firstborn from the dead; that in all *things* he might have the preeminence. [19] For it pleased *the Father* that in him should all fulness dwell" (Colossians 1:12-19).

Paul writes with some very vivid Jewish imagery (v. 12). There are certain words in the text that are *key words* to that imagery such as "inheritance" and "saints in light." The word "inheritance" refers to something *assigned* or *allotted*. These words would immediately draw the attention of the twelve tribes of Israel to the *Land of Promise*. These words meant a *kingdom* for them.

However, the *kingdom* Paul refers to in this imagery is the *kingdom* "in light" - the realm of *absolute truth* ("saints in light," v. 12). This *kingdom* is the realm of God's sovereignty, glory, and grace. It is the realm where truth reigns supreme and where the living Word of God is Lord.

This *kingdom* "of light" is the heavenly presence of God that fills the universe. It extends to the uttermost parts of the universe in both the *macro* and *micro* sense of existence. The *kingdom* "of light" is another dimension of existence that transcends time and space, yet our time and space are a part of this existence. Although this other existence is beyond our human senses (I Corinthians 2:9), all believers are intended to live in this reality by grace through faith. We presently live in this invisible existence as we yield to the Holy Spirit and are empowered to live in obedience to God's revealed will (truth) in the Word of God. This invisible existence is the *kingdom* where Jesus is Lord.

All believers have been qualified to live in this realm by the finished work of Christ. They are enabled to succeed in this realm by the enabling grace of God through the indwelling presence of the Holy Spirit in their life. We must be careful to emphasize that this realm of "light" that Christ has qualified the believer to live in is a *spiritual realm*. We can participate in it only when we are fully surrendered to the Spirit of God in us (Romans 6:11-13). Only the Holy Spirit can live God's truth through us. We cannot succeed in this spiritual existence apart from the enabling of the indwelling Holy Spirit of God. This is to what the words "made meet" in Colossians 1:12 refer.

When the Word of God uses the word "saints," it refers to individuals "born again" of the Spirit of God. The "saints" are those who have been set apart from this world and have become part of this heavenly existence. "Saints" refers to beings fit to live in the presence of God. Every Christian should understand that we live in this existence *now*. It is not a *pie in the sky* thing. It is our present reality. This fact ought to change the way we think and live in this world.

"[17] Brethren, be followers together of me, and mark them which walk so as ye have us for an ensample. [18] (For many walk, of whom I have told you often, and now tell you even weeping, *that they are* the enemies of the cross of Christ: [19] Whose end *is* destruction, whose God *is their* belly, and *whose* glory *is* in their shame, who mind earthly things.) [20] For our conversation is in heaven; from whence also we look for the Saviour, the Lord Jesus Christ: [21] Who shall change our vile body, that it may be fashioned like unto his glorious body, according to the working whereby he is able even to subdue all things unto himself" (Philippians 3:17-21).

The word "conversation" in Philippians 3:20 is from the Greek word *politeuma* (pol-it'-yoo-mah). It refers to a citizenship in a commonwealth governed and administrated by laws (in this case, the laws of God). This is the believer's present reality of existence.

The second imagery: the conquering *Deliverer* (v. 13).

For the apostate Jew, salvation came by *pleasing* God through works. For the pagan, salvation came by *appeasing* their god(s) with self-flagellation, human sacrifices, 0etc. In the Hellenization of the Jews, these two ideas became merged and were integrated into Judaism.

To the Christian, salvation came wrapped in a package and offered as a gift to be received by faith. To the early Christians, allowing anything to pervert the Gospel of a *finished* work of redemption offered as a *gift* was a crime that disqualified a person from participating in the *kingdom* of "light" (the realm where the truth of God's Word reigns supreme). The Gospel is the *key* to that Kingdom.

"[13] When Jesus came into the coasts of Caesarea Philippi, he asked his disciples, saying, Whom do men say that I the Son of man am? [14] And they said, Some *say that thou art* John the Baptist: some, Elias; and others, Jeremias, or one of the prophets. [15] He saith unto them, But whom say ye that I am? [16] And Simon Peter answered and said, Thou art the Christ, the Son of the living God. [17] And Jesus answered and said unto him, Blessed art thou, Simon Barjona: for flesh and blood hath not revealed *it* unto thee, but my Father which is in heaven. [18] And I say also unto thee, That thou art Peter {*petros - little stone*}, and upon this rock {*Peter's profession of faith; petra – large rock or cliff; the city carved from a rock cliff was known as Petra*} I will build my church; and the gates of hell shall not prevail against it. [19] And I will give unto thee the keys of the kingdom of heaven: and whatsoever thou shalt bind on earth shall be bound in heaven: and whatsoever thou shalt loose on earth shall be loosed in heaven" (Matthew 16:13-19).

These truths were a direct contradiction to the Gnosticism that was perverting early Christianity. Gnostics taught that salvation came through a process of enlightenment in varying levels of spiritual knowledge (the *stairway to heaven* heresy). In Gnostics' corrupted view of salvation, God did not *give* a person salvation. A person *achieved* salvation.

According to Colossians 1:14 ("In whom we have redemption"), the Father's work is complete. The Father has *once for all* qualified, rescued, and transferred the believer into His "kingdom . . . of light." Delivery from the *tyranny of darkness* is a *finished* work of God and part of the believer's present reality. Nothing can be added, or needs to be added, to what the Father has done. "In Christ," we presently possess redemption "through His blood." In other words, our redemption was a costly liberation.

"Forgiveness" (Colossians 1:14) is not overlooking the problem of sin. Forgiveness is available because the *penalty* (God's *judgment* upon sin, Romans 6:23a) has already been paid. Forgiveness is a benefit of salvation, not that which procures it. The word "forgiveness" in Colossians 1:14 is from the Greek word *aphesis* (af'-es-is), which means to *release from bondage or imprisonment* - to *remit the penalty.* When a believer understands the Gospel and rests in Christ's finished work, the remission of his death sentence is part of the gift of his salvation.

"Forgiveness" is the by-product of redemption (the "wages" of sin being paid). Therefore, forgiveness is the *remission of a deserved penalty* because that penalty has been already substitutionally paid in the sacrifice of Jesus Christ. "Forgiveness" is not just God treating the believer like sin never happened. Forgiveness is not *painting over* our sin like we would paint over a dirty word on the wall. The remission of sin is removing any evidence that the sin was ever there. Our condemning sin was there at one time, but now it is completely gone.

When we consider what the Bible teaches on the *Kingdom of Heaven* and the *Kingdom of God*, we must be careful that we do not enter into the confusion of the heretical Theonomic view of the kingdom. The Theonomic view of the kingdom is the outcome of *Replacement Theology* wherein the nation of Israel is replaced with a universal, one world church that will rule over the world after they usher in a utopian society. This kingdom view is very similar to the distorted view of most of the Jews at the time of Christ's incarnation. They saw the kingdom as material, earthly, and political. Although the Kingdom of Heaven will always be material to some degree, the true Kingdom of God is purely spiritual and eternal. The Kingdom of Heaven is a *creation dominion* (Lordship). The Kingdom of God encompasses the Kingdom of Heaven and is inclusive of the *creation dominion.* God's sovereignty encompasses both the Kingdom of Heaven (His creation) and the Kingdom of God (His eternal existence).

In Colossians 1:15-19, we now move away from Christ's accomplishment in His work of redemption to *who He is.* In verse nineteen, "fullness" refers to all that God is or possesses now residing in Jesus Christ through His incarnation. This refers especially to His sovereign authority in His Lordship. These verses portray the *sovereign position* of Jesus over all other realities in all other existences. The focal statement is in verse eighteen - "That in **everything** He might have pre-eminence."

All worship of God *must* focus upon Jesus and His work. It is not enough to intellectually recognize that Jesus excels and is sovereignly above all other humans. We must personally give Him *preeminence* in our lives. The purpose of this statement is to expand upon the person who Jesus is. He is not merely the Father's *angelic agent* in the work of redemption as the Gnostics believed. He is God's agent in the whole of God's workings from creation to the consummation of history.

"[5] Let this mind be in you, which was also in Christ Jesus: [6] Who, being in the form of God, thought it not robbery to be equal with God: [7] But made himself of no reputation, and took upon him the form of a servant, and was made in the likeness of men: [8] And being found in fashion as a man, he humbled himself, and became obedient unto death, even the death of the cross. [9] Wherefore God also hath highly exalted him, and given him a name which is above every name: [10] That at the name of Jesus every knee should bow, of *things* in heaven, and *things* in earth, and *things* under the earth; [11] And *that* every tongue should confess that Jesus Christ *is* Lord, to the glory of God the Father" (Philippians 2:5-11).

The Father *plans*. The Son *executes* that plan. The Spirit is the *power* of execution. The Lordship of Jesus in Colossians 1:15-19 is twofold:

1. He is the Lord of the fallen creation (vs.15-17).
2. He is the Lord of the *New Creation* (the church - vs.18-19).

Christ's sovereignty is described. In Colossians 1:15, Jesus is described as "the image of the invisible God." "Image" is not just a reflection of likeness. If you were able to take a photograph of the "invisible God," the image that would be seen would be Jesus Christ. The image would also reveal all of God's attributes and spiritual characteristics. In other words, Jesus is God.

"He that hath seen me {*Jesus*} has seen the Father" (John 14:9).

In Colossians 1:18, Jesus is also referred to as "the firstborn of all creation." This does not refer to Jesus being the first to be created. "Firstborn" is a Hebraism - a Hebrew phrase, idiom, or custom which can only be understood by understanding the idiom or custom. The word "firstborn" spoke of holding a position of priority. The legal term is *primogeniture*. Therefore, the "firstborn" was usually the oldest in the family and resultantly held the patriarchal position of priority ("preeminence," Colossians 1:18) upon the father's death.

"[27] Also I will make him *my* firstborn, higher than the kings of the earth. [28] My mercy will I keep for him for evermore, and my covenant shall stand fast with him. [29] His seed also will I make *to endure* for ever, and his throne as the days of heaven" (Psalm 89:27-29).

44

Therefore, Christ Jesus possesses this *position* as the "last Adam" (I Corinthians 15:45) and as the new *Federal Head* of the *New Creation.* He holds these positions of *preeminence* because He is the "image of God," or is in essence God. The first Adam was created in the "image of God," but that image was defaced in his fall through the corruption of sin.

Since none of His creation is older than the Creator, He holds the first patriarchal position of priority (v.16). He will always be the Sovereign of sovereigns (Lord of lords). He restores *creation dominion* to humanity by becoming part of His creation when He was born as a baby. "Image" refers to Jesus being a physical revelation of the "invisible God." Again, this would be a complete contradiction against the teachings of Gnosticism. Gnosticism taught that the spiritual can never exist together with the material.

"Firstborn" refers to, and amplifies, the fact that even though Jesus had a physical birth, He is *eternally preexistent*. According to Colossians 1:17, Jesus brought the material creation into existence. The material world was also created completely dependent upon Him for its continuing existence ("by him all things consist').

THE SCOPE OF CREATION – v. 16
"All things" (universally - material and spiritual)
Jesus is Lord of it all.

"Whether they be thrones, or dominions, or principalities or powers," He is Lord of *all*. "In heaven," He is Lord of the angels. In earth, He is Lord (Sovereign) over men, animals, and the natural laws of physics. He is Lord of the "visible" things we can see. He is Lord of the "invisible" things we cannot see, such as angels and the souls of men.

The Colossian Church was under attack by the philosophy of the Gnostics. The Gnostics believed in angel worship - that there were various levels of angelic beings that *filled the gap* between God and man (the spiritual and material worlds). They also believed that they were dependent upon these angels as a medium for communion with God. This later developed into praying through *saints* in Catholicism (the angels that the Gnostics prayed *through* to get to God were replaced by *saints)*. This *Catholic heresy* is no less wrong than the *Gnostic heresy*. The *Catholic heresy* has just become more acceptable. Paul immediately eradicated all these mediators between the spiritual world and the physical (material) world and points them to the one Mediator, Jesus Christ.

THE LORD OF THE NEW CREATION
Colossians 1:18-19
His Body - the Church

In Colossians 1:15-17, the emphasis is on the *eternal person* of Jesus. In Colossians 1:18-19, the emphasis turns to the present resurrected glory of the incarnate One. Jesus is Lord of the "church of the firstborn" (Hebrews 12:23, which are the "first fruits" of the New Creation). The "church of the firstborn" is made up of all people who have put their faith in the *finished work* of Christ for their salvation since the Day of Pentecost (both living and dead believers). They have already been "born again" into this "kingdom . . . of light." The word "church" also refers to the future resurrected and glorified body of believers that will rule and reign with Christ during His one-thousand year reign on earth. However, the "kingdom . . . of light" is their present reality of existence within this material world.

Jesus is "the beginning" (Colossians1:18) of this *New Creation*. The emphasis of this text is not on the "church," but on "the regeneration" to this *new life* (existence). Jesus is the beginning of the *New Creation* as the eternal God-man.

"Therefore if any man *be* in Christ, *he is* a new creature: old things are passed away; behold, all things are become new" (II Corinthians 5:17).

Jesus is the *firstborn out from among the dead* into this *New Creation*. What man sees as an end, God sees as a *new beginning*.

> "[51] Behold, I shew you a mystery; We shall not all sleep, but we shall all be changed, [52] In a moment, in the twinkling of an eye, at the last trump: for the trumpet shall sound, and the dead shall be raised incorruptible, and we shall be changed. [53] For this corruptible must put on incorruption, and this mortal *must* put on immortality. [54] So when this corruptible shall have put on incorruption, and this mortal shall have put on immortality, then shall be brought to pass the saying that is written, Death is swallowed up in victory. [55] O death, where *is* thy sting? O grave, where *is* thy victory? [56] The sting of death *is* sin; and the strength of sin *is* the law. [57] But thanks *be* to God, which giveth us the victory through our Lord Jesus Christ" (I Corinthians 15:51-57).

It would be of little value to be Lord of a *dead creation*. Therefore, Jesus died so we could become part of His *New Creation*. "All things" refers to both the spiritual and material universe including the "church." The words "might have pre-eminence" means Jesus is made firstborn, sovereign, and LORD. This happens in this present worldly existence when individual believers chose Jesus as their Sovereign. This is what the word "might" means in Colossians 1:18.

Today, He does not force his Lordship on a world that does not want Him or who refuse to yield to His will. If He is practically the Lord of your universe, then you have yielded to Him. He is Lord! However, if you want to be qualified by Him to participate in His *realm of light*, you will have to practically bring your life under His Lordship. Have you yielded to Him as the *one* and *only* Lord of your existence?

Jesus is Lord!

Studies in the Epistle to the Colossians
Chapter Four
THE SOVEREIGNTY OF JESUS IN HIS PRESENT KINGDOM OF LIGHT

1. To what does the word "inheritance" refer in Colossians 1:12 regarding the Church?

2. What kind of a realm is the "kingdom" of Christ presently?

3. From Colossians 1:13, what is the second imagery Paul is conveying?

4. What is the *key* that opens the door of salvation and allows the believer participation in the Kingdom of the Spirit of truth?

5. What is the significance of Colossians 1:14?

6. According to Colossians 1:15-19, what position does Christ presently occupy (what resides in Him)?

7. What is the twofold Lordship of Jesus?

8. Discuss the meaning of "the image of the invisible God." How can you have an image of something invisible?

9. What does the Hebraism "firstborn" mean as it refers to Jesus Christ?

10. What is the purpose of the statement of Colossians 1:16-17 about the influence of the Gnostics at Colosse? How is this relevant to today?

11. In Colossians 1:18-19, Jesus is portrayed as the Lord of the New Creation. What is the biblical term for the group of people that presently make up the New Creation?

12. What does it mean when verse 18 says, Jesus is "the beginning"?

Jesus is Lord!

Studies in the Epistle to the Colossians
Chapter Five
LIVING ON THE ROCK CHRIST JESUS

"[19] For it pleased the Father that in him should all fulness dwell; [20] And, having made peace through the blood of his cross, by him to reconcile all things unto himself; by him, I say, whether they be things in earth, or things in heaven. [21] And you, that were sometime alienated and enemies in your mind by wicked works, yet now hath he reconciled [22] In the body of his flesh through death, to present you holy and unblameable and unreproveable in his sight: [23] If ye continue in the faith grounded and settled, and be not moved away from the hope of the gospel, which ye have heard, and which was preached to every creature which is under heaven; whereof I Paul am made a minister" (Colossians 1:19-23).

In verse nineteen, the word translated "fullness" was understood and used by the Gnostics to denote various *mediatorial images* that were each believed to give a partial revelation of God. Therefore, it was necessary to have "knowledge" of all these *mediators* in order to have a *full knowledge* of God.

When Paul told Timothy (I Timothy 2:5) that Christ was the only "mediator between God and men," he was denying the whole foundation of Gnostic beliefs. Some continue a form of Gnosticism in praying (invocation) to saints, angels, the dead, and to Mary. There are two primary characteristics of Christ's "fullness" of the Godhead.

1. In Jesus we find the totality of divine powers and attributes. Everything that God is, Jesus is.
2. The "fullness of the Godhead" dwells "in Christ." This "fullness" is the *permanent residence.* of the fullness of the Godhead in Christ Jesus. The idea conveys the permanency of the union of God and man in the person of Jesus.

The fullness of the Godhead "in Christ" is a provision for mankind's benefit (Colossians 1:20-23). Again, the Gnostics taught that there could only be a partial completion of the work of salvation. Therefore, a person could never be fully saved, because the angelic *mediators* could only provide a *partial reconciliation.* The emphasis of verses 20-23 is that the security of a believer's salvation is based upon an already accomplished reality. Jesus has provided *complete reconciliation* to God.

Because Christ Jesus is fully God and fully man, He becomes the only true possible "mediator between God and men." This refers to the new *Federal Headship* of the New Creation in Jesus Christ. Jesus is fully able to reconcile man to God, not just partially as the Gnostics taught. He is able to do this because this *New Mediator* is both God and man. The *totality* of the work of Christ provides two basics *absolutely.*

1. "Peace" - it means to bind together that which was separated. This is a *finished reality* for the believer.
2. "Reconcile" - it means the restoration to the original fellowship that Adam enjoyed before the fall. Presently a person can only have this fellowship with God "in Christ."

Both "peace" and "reconciliation" rest upon an eternally satisfactory and completed work *accomplished by God Himself.* Therefore, salvation provides a *position* of *eternal security* for the believer who has absolutely trusted in that finished work of Jesus.

Three Observations about the Fullness of Reconciliation II Corinthians 5:18-21

"[18] And all things are of God, who hath reconciled us to himself by Jesus Christ, and hath given to us the ministry of reconciliation; [19] To wit, that God was in Christ, reconciling the world unto himself, not imputing their trespasses unto them; and hath committed unto us the word of reconciliation. [20] Now then we are ambassadors for Christ, as though God did beseech you by us: we pray you in Christ's stead, be ye reconciled to God. [21] For he hath made him to be sin for us, who knew no sin; that we might be made the righteousness of God in him" (II Corinthians 5:18-21).

1. II Corinthians 5:19 - God initiated the blood sacrifice and provided Himself as the sacrifice.

"[17] Therefore doth my Father love me, because I lay down my life, that I might take it again. [18] No man taketh it from me, but I lay it down of myself. I have power to lay it down, and I have power to take it again. This commandment have I received of my Father" (John 10:17-18).

The sacrifice of Christ is both offered to God and provided by God. Therefore, we can be confident that the sacrifice meets all of God's requirements to satisfy His expectations. Jesus is both the perfect *Offerer* and the perfect *offering* (Hebrews 10:12).

2. II Corinthians 5:21 - The Father provided the Son as the *substitute sin bearer.* In the death of the crucifixion at Calvary, Jesus bore *all* of God's wrath and judgment upon all sin (compare I John 2:2, I Peter 2:24, and 3:18).

3. II Corinthians 5:20 - Since God's entire wrath against sin has been satisfied, there is no barrier on God's side to hinder man's complete reconciliation. Therefore, the only barrier is on man's side, because he is unwilling to trust absolutely.

Because of the "fullness" of Jesus, the believer has the fullness of reconciliation. The believer is *fully, totally,* and *absolutely* bound to God *eternally* ("peace"). The believer is *fully, totally,* and *absolutely* restored to God *eternally* ("reconciled").

THE PAST AND PRESENT
Colossians 1:21

1. Past (when the Colossian believers were lost)

The word "alienated" is from the Greek word *apallotrioo* (ap-al-lot-ree-o'-o). It means to be shut out from fellowship or intimacy. The unsaved man is *estranged* from God.

"Enemies" is from the Greek word *echthros* (ech-thros'). It means to be hateful or hostile. It means to be a bitter enemy. We see that this hostility towards God is in the "minds" of all lost men. "Mind" is from the Greek word *dianoia* (dee-an'-oy-ah). It refers to man's imaginations. It refers to the mind as a faculty of understanding, feeling, and desiring.

> "Because that, when they knew God, they glorified him not as God, neither were thankful; but became vain in their imaginations, and their foolish heart was darkened" (Romans 1:21).

"Wicked" is from the Greek word *poneros* (pon-ay-ros') and refers to a broad category of evil practices or things. "Works" is from the Greek word *ergon* (er'-gon) and refers to the things in life with which one occupies his time. These two words reveal the arena of the exhibition of this person's alienation and hostility toward God.

2. Present (once the Colossian believers were "born again")

The saved are now in a new state of existence with God. They are "reconciled." The word "reconciled" is from the Greek word *apokatallasso* (ap-ok-at-al-las'-so). It means to completely restore someone to a former state of harmony. The "born again" believer is no longer an alien or foreigner. The Colossian believers became "citizens of heaven" once they were "born again."

> "For our conversation is in heaven; from whence also we look for the Saviour, the Lord Jesus Christ" (Philippians 3:20).

THE FOURFOLD POSITION OF THE BELIEVER BEFORE GOD "IN CHRIST"

There are four statements in Colossians 1:22 that expand upon this *new existence* in which the believer presently lives. By salvation (regeneration; i.e. re-creation), the believer has completely changed his position before God. Regeneration removes us from the fallen first creation in Adam and immerses the believer in the New Creation "in Christ." This is known as the "baptism of the Spirit" (I Corinthians 12:13). These four statements reveal what Christ has accomplished for the believer in this New Creation "in the body of His flesh through death."

"Holy" is from the Greek word *hagios* (hag'-ee-os). The most fundamental idea of the word is separation unto God's service. It can also refer to something, or someone distinctively separated from everything other than God's use. When God commands the believer to "be holy," He is commanding the believer to become *practically* what he is *positionally* already "in Christ." *Practically* "holy" refers to the believer's new *position* as "priests" before God (I Peter 2:9-12).

> "[14] As obedient children, not fashioning yourselves according to the former lusts in your ignorance: [15] But as he which hath called you is holy, so be ye holy in all manner of conversation; [16] Because it is written, Be ye holy; for I am holy" (I Peter 1:14-16).

"Unblameable" is from the Greek word *amomos* (am'-o-mos). It means *without any fault* such as a sacrificial animal that had been inspected closely for disease and was found to be without any defect or blemish. "In Christ," every believer is perfectly faultless, without blemish, and morally pure.

"Unreprovable" is from the Greek word *anegkletos* (an-eng'-klay-tos). It means *irreproachable* and *unaccusable*. "In Christ," there is nothing about us, or anything in our sin account for which we can be accused before God. We are what Christ is in the eyes of the Father.

"In His sight" brings us into the realm of these other three statements. The believer is "holy," "unblameable," and "unreprovable" "in His sight." This refers to the omniscient vision of God from which nothing can be hidden. This refers to the *microscopic* and *macroscopic* vision of God that sees everything at every level of its existence. Yet, "in christ," He finds the believer perfect in every sense.

DEFINING SAVING FAITH - Colossians 1:23

The word "if" is not a contingency for salvation. The warning is for heretics who would prove their own unbelief by following false beliefs similar to the beliefs of the Gnostics. False beliefs keep people from being saved "by grace through faith."

The Gnostics believed that they needed to personally participate in their salvation by their own added works and by the invocation of angelic beings as mediators. Salvation was something to be *achieved*, not *received*. For the Gnostic, salvation came through *achieving* various degrees of enlightenment (knowledge) revealed to them though visions from a host of intermediaries.

Retaining salvation is not in question (obviously from the context). What is in question is if these individuals will abandon the objective facts of the Gospel message. This rejection would be manifested by doctrines contradicting the Gospel. This rejection would be manifested by accepting or following the false teachings of Gnosticism and by continuing in worldly practices. Doing so would manifest that there was no real faith with which to begin. The logic is that no one who truly understands and believes a pure Gospel of grace would ever abandon it.

"Continue" is from the Greek word *epimeno* (ep-ee-men'-o). It means to stay with or live in the inscripturalized truths of God's Word ("the faith'). Continuation is a proof that real saving faith has been placed in the work of Christ. "Continue" means to *stay with* something and not abandon it. "The faith" refers to the practice of the body of truth or system of beliefs that were delivered to the believer in the Word of God.

"[5] One Lord, one faith, one baptism, [6] One God and Father of all, who is above all, and through all, and in you all" (Ephesians 4:5-6).

"Grounded and settled" refers to *practice* of "the faith" that is foundational to a life style based upon a solid conviction that what is presented by God's Word is absolute truth. If that is the case, that conviction will be "settled." In other words, it will result in a permanent confidence and a practical reality of a living faith.

THE ADMONITION OF THE FAITH

"Be not moved away" from the foundational truths in the Gospel of an absolutely complete, finished, and satisfactory work of redemption "in Christ" (I Corinthians 15:58). Gnosticism is a *fluid* philosophy that is constantly adding new requirements to man's journey to his own *divinity*. Gnosticism has evolved to the place where every man must find his own pathway to *God(hood)*. This shifting sand of relativistic, ecumenical, and false theology has undermined the "faith" of many people. These people are easily moved when they are not "grounded and settled" in the sufficiency of the sacrifice of Christ and in the understanding of the reality of their new existence "in Christ."

FOR ALL WHO WILL TRUST IN HIM, CHRIST JESUS HAS LAID A FIRM FOUNDATION ON WHICH TO SETTLE THEIR LIVES. HAVE YOU MOVED INTO YOUR HOUSE ON THE ROCK, OR ARE YOU JUST STANDING OUTSIDE LOOKING IN THE WINDOW?

Jesus is Lord!

Studies in the Epistle to the Colossians
Chapter Five
LIVING ON THE ROCK CHRIST JESUS

1. From Colossians 1:19, what did the word translated "fullness" mean to the early Gnostics?

2. How is Paul's use of "fullness" regarding Jesus Christ intended to correct this heresy?

3. What are the two characteristics of Christ's fullness?

4. How do the truths of Colossians 1:20-23 correct the heretical teaching that the work of salvation is only partially completed and that no one can be fully saved?

5. What two words from Colossians 1:20 reveal the two absolute provisions of Christ's work of salvation? Define them and discuss what they mean in relation to the believer.

6. Give the three observations about the fullness of reconciliation from II Corinthians 5:18-21.

7. What three statements from Colossians 1:21 reveal the believer's *past* relationship to God?

8. What four statements from Colossians 1:22 reveal how our Savior presents us to the Father?

Jesus is Lord!

Studies in the Epistle to the Colossians
Chapter Six
THE ANALYSIS OF CHRISTIAN SERVICE

"[24] Who now rejoice in my sufferings for you, and fill up that which is behind of the afflictions of Christ in my flesh for his body's sake, which is the church: [25] Whereof I am made a minister, according to the dispensation of God which is given to me for you, to fulfil the word of God; [26] Even the mystery which hath been hid from ages and from generations, but now is made manifest to his saints: [27] To whom God would make known what is the riches of the glory of this mystery among the Gentiles; which is Christ in you, the hope of glory: [28] Whom we preach, warning every man, and teaching every man in all wisdom; that we may present every man perfect in Christ Jesus: [29] Whereunto I also labour, striving according to his working, which worketh in me mightily" (Colossians 1:24-29).

In Colossians 1:23, Paul said he was made a "minister" of the Gospel. What is a "minister"? The word is translated from the Greek word *diakonos* (dee-ak'-on-os). The primary meaning of the word is to be a *servant*. We cannot separate the obligation of this service from the Lordship of Jesus Christ. If we call Him Lord, we are obligated to serve Him.

All the various Gnostic sects promised salvation through an occult knowledge that they claimed was revealed to them through *intermediary eternal beings*. These *intermediary eternal beings,* or Messengers of Light (*Aeons*), were sent to them from the *Pleroma* (the divine realm of the gods). It was believed that they were sent to restore the *lost knowle*dge (Gnosis) of humanity's divine origin. Salvation was a restoration of individuals to this *divine order* (similar to modern *Christian Reconstructionism*).

However, like all cults, salvation was *achieved*, not *received*. Gnostic salvation is nothing more than spiritual freedom from a physical existence. Physical existence is viewed as a predicament from which a person must *escape* through *enlightenment*. In Gnosticism, man needs to be saved from the consequences of ignorance of his own divinity, not from the consequences of sin (condemnation and death). Within *Christian* Gnosticism, Jesus was the Savior. Jesus was not the Savior because He propitiated God through His substitutionary sacrifice at Calvary, but through His *teachings*. These *teachings* were viewed as mysteries to be understood allegorically. Gnosis (salvation) needed to be stimulated by the Messengers of Light (*Aeons*) as they moved the pilgrim along the pathway to his *enlightenment*. These Messengers of Light established salvific mysteries (sacraments) that could be administered by their apostles (clergymen) as their successors (*Sacerdotal Successionism*).

As an individual advanced through the various *stages* (*levels - aeons*) of Gnosis, that individual advanced himself in status among his peers seeking to be restored to the realm of the divine order. Salvation was the ultimate Gnosis - *pleroma*. Individuals were viewed as being closer to their own *godhood* as they moved upward in these various degrees of knowledge. This *knowledge* (Gnosis) was the *divine life*. *Enlightenment* brought the pilgrim slowly along on his journey to his own *divinity*. The Gnostic search for God turns the seeker's attention towards his own *inner being*. The modern Gnostic does not seek salvation in either the inspired or incarnate Word of God. He seeks salvation in the metaphysics of *Jungian Depth Psychology*.

This all seems so complex and so foreign to anyone understanding the simplicity of God's plan of redemption. God has chosen to use the "born again" human agent to bring the knowledge of Christ and His work to the lost world. God has ordained the local church to be His vehicle for the communication of the Gospel to the lost world. He does this as the "saints" are equipped to do the "work of the ministry" through their local church.

Diakonos was a general term applied to those engaged in service of any sort, especially and distinctively the seemingly menial work of a being a bond-servant. In the world, the word "servant" distinguished an individual as the lowest of social orders. However, it became a common identification for the early Christians. The words "minister" (*diakonos*) and "servant" (*doulos*) were used interchangeably for Christians.

"[42] But Jesus called them to him, and saith unto them, Ye know that they which are accounted to rule over the Gentiles exercise lordship over them; and their great ones exercise authority upon them. [43] But so shall it not be among you: but whosoever will be great among you, shall be your minister {*diakonos*}: [44] And whosoever of you will be the chiefest, shall be servant {*doulos*} of all. [45] For even the Son of man came not to be ministered {*diakoneo*} unto, but to minister {*diakoneo*}, and to give his life a ransom for many" (Mark 10:42-45; compare Romans 1:1; Philippians. 2:7; Titus 1:1; James 1:1; II Peter 1:1; Jude 1:1).

These two words (minister and servant) describe the attitude of Christian service. This attitude involves two details of life:

1. The renunciation of a person's individual rights and freedoms
2. The commitment to a life of lowly service

THE PRESSURES OF SERVICE

"Who" in Colossians 1:24 is better translated "I." "Who" refers to Paul. Christian service should carry with it an attitude of rejoicing, but there are many stepping stones through the fire within Christian service. Ministry comes with many *fiery trials*. This is what Paul refers to by the use of the word "afflictions." "Afflictions" is translated from the Greek word *thlipsis* (thlip'-sis). It simply means pressure. Paul was realizing humiliation in his own life similar to the suffering with which Christ was humiliated before His crucifixion. These pressures of the ministry come in the forms of rejection, ridicule, and various degrees of persecution.

The result of these *pressures* on the ministering saint is "sufferings" (Colossians 1:24). We do not rejoice because of sufferings. We can rejoice in the midst of them. We endure sufferings because of the hope of the realization of salvation and maturity in the lives of those we have chosen to serve.

> "[1] Wherefore seeing we also are compassed about with so great a cloud of witnesses, let us lay aside every weight, and the sin which doth so easily beset us, and let us run with patience the race that is set before us, [2] Looking unto Jesus the author and finisher of our faith; who for the joy that was set before him endured the cross, despising the shame, and is set down at the right hand of the throne of God. [3] For consider him that endured such contradiction of sinners against himself, lest ye be wearied and faint in your minds. [4] Ye have not yet resisted unto blood, striving against sin" (Hebrews 12:1-4).

Seeking to live righteously for righteousness' sake and for truth's sake will eventually bring persecution ("Yea, and all that will live godly in Christ Jesus shall suffer persecution" - II Timothy 3:12). Being a Christ-like servant will demand enormous amounts of time and will frequently be exhausting. We will suffer emotionally due to the resistance to truth by those we serve and the persecution from those who resist.

THE PURPOSE OF SERVICE - "For his body's sake, which is the church" (Colossians 1:24)

The purpose of service is for the "body's sake" (the "body" of which Christ is "head"). It is only by serving the "body" that we anoint the "head."

> "[12] For the perfecting of the saints, for the work of the ministry, for the edifying of the body of Christ: . . . [16] From whom the whole body fitly joined together and compacted by that which every joint supplieth, according to the effectual working in the measure of every part, maketh increase of the body unto the edifying of itself in love" (Ephesians 4:12 and 16).

THE ELEMENTS OF SERVICE (Colossians 1:25)

Paul was made a "minister" or servant of the local church, the body of Christ. All ministry is to be done through the local church. Any ministry that is not *umbilicalized* to the local church is unbiblical. The local church is the "household of God" (not *house*, but "household;" Ephesians 2:19). All of the collective family members are under one patriarch - Christ Jesus.

This is "according to the dispensation of God" - *The Law of the Household.* The idea here is stewardship and faithfulness to a biblical mandate. As an Apostle, Paul was to administrate the laws that regulated the proper conduct of God's "household" (now in local churches).

This was to be done in order "to fulfill the Word of God" (Colossians 1:25). This refers to a complete and full understanding of God's *plan*, *program*, and *purpose*. Paul's goal was to bring all those under his care into the perimeters defined by God's *plan*, *program*, and *purpose*. This involves two responsibilities for the servant.

1. The accurate communication of God's Word in the message and ideas the message conveys

2. Personal obedience to that which is learned or taught

THE "MYSTERY" OF GENTILE SERVICE (Colossians 1:26)

There was something hidden in the Scriptures from the previous generations, especially the Jew. That does not mean it was not there, but that God did not give them understanding of its meaning. That "mystery" was the free admission of Gentiles to the promises of the Abrahamic Covenant.

"[1] For this cause I Paul, the prisoner of Jesus Christ for you Gentiles, [2] If ye have heard of the dispensation of the grace of God which is given me to you–ward: [3] How that by revelation he made known unto me the mystery; (as I wrote afore in few words, [4] Whereby, when ye read, ye may understand my knowledge in the mystery of Christ) [5] Which in other ages was not made known unto the sons of men, as it is now revealed unto his holy apostles and prophets by the Spirit; [6] That the Gentiles should be fellowheirs, and of the same body, and partakers of his promise in Christ by the gospel: [7] Whereof I was made a minister, according to the gift of the grace of God given unto me by the effectual working of his power. [8] Unto me, who am less than the least of all saints, is this grace given, that I should preach among the Gentiles the unsearchable riches of Christ; [9] And to make all men see what is the fellowship of the mystery, which from the beginning of the world hath been hid in God, who created all things by Jesus Christ: [10] To the intent that now unto the principalities and powers in heavenly places might be known by the church the manifold wisdom of God, [11] According to the eternal purpose which he purposed in Christ Jesus our Lord: [12] In whom we have boldness and access with confidence by the faith of him" (Ephesians 3:1-12).

Therefore, any Gentile should considered it a great privileged to be able to serve God. Somehow people think that because they have submitted their lives to serving that they are doing God a *favor*. In reality, it is God who shows the servant grace by allowing sinners to serve in any capacity. This is what is meant by the words "the riches of His glory among the Gentiles."

The preaching of the Gospel to the Gentiles brought forth "abundant" fruit. "Riches" signifies that it produced an overwhelming harvest of servants. The purpose of evangelism is not to simply produce *souls*, but to produce *servants* (Matthew 28:20).

THE METHODOLOGY OF SERVICE (Colossians 1:28)
Methodology is the study of methods and means.

Colossians 1:28: (Jesus) "whom we preach" - a system of Christian doctrine is powerless unless it centers on the *Lordship* of its giver. *Lordship* reveals submission to the giver of truth and to the truth that is given. Therefore, to teach the body of truth revealed to us by Jesus as His representative servant is to convey His message - not ours. In doing so, we "preach Jesus."

"Warnings" and "teaching" - it is essential that the servant has a balanced exhortation of God's Word "in all wisdom." People need to be warned of the danger they are in if they will not study to know and obey God's Word. People need to be taught (or corrected) when they wander into areas where they ought not to be. It is cruelty, not kindness, which does not deal with people who continue in their rebellious wanderings.

Wisdom is the *heart* and *mind* of God operating in the life of the believer. Therefore, "warnings and teaching" must direct those wandering outside of the *circle of truth* back into the will of God.

THE INTENTION OF MINISTRY (Colossians 1:28)

The *end to the means* is "that we present every man perfect in Christ Jesus." The central focus of God's message is not on *quantity*, but *quality*. All too often Christian growth is measured only in numbers, not in *depth*. The true objective of Christian service is growth in depth, not in size. Size will be the natural product of depth. It is not enough to bring a person to a profession of faith. The labor of service is to bring him to full maturity. Ask any mother, she will tell you that her real labor was not in giving birth to a child, but the two decades that followed.

THE LABOR OF SERVICE (Colossians 1:29)

Ministry that takes the Lord seriously, both in knowing His Word and practicing it, is hard work. "Labour" in Colossians 1:29 is from the Greek word *kopiao* (kop-ee-ah'-o). It means to be weary with toil or burdens of grief. The word "striving" is from the Greek word *agonizomai* (ag-o-nid'-zom-ahee). It means to labor to the point of exhaustion or to agonize in effort. "Striving" refers to the spiritual struggle of ministry using the last ounce of one's energy to bring a person to salvation and spiritual maturity.

Few people are willing to put this kind of effort into their own spiritual growth, let alone into the spiritual growth of others. Laboring to serve others and to help them grow spiritually is one of the best ways to promote our own spiritual growth.

THE POWER OF SERVICE - "According to His working" (Colossians 1:29)

"Working" is from the Greek word *energeia* (en-erg'-i-ah). In the New Testament, it is only used of a *supernatural power* (God's or of demons). God wants to supernaturally empower each believer for ministry. This supernatural empowering is essential to fruitful ministry.

Paul labored, not in his own strength, but in the strength of the indwelling Christ. In his own strength, Paul would have given up the struggle to bring believers to maturity. Because of the enabling power of the indwelling Holy Spirit, Paul was able to keep on fighting and struggling for the establishment of truth in the lives of believers (and it is a battle).

This is what Paul refers to by the words, "which worketh in me mightily" (or *powerfully*). The strength of Christ is not something the believer needs to plead with God to receive. The strength of Christ is naturally and inherently available to any *obedient believer*.

"Whereby are given unto us exceeding great and precious promises: that by these ye might be partakers of the divine nature, having escaped the corruption that is in the world through lust" (II Peter 1:4).

Jesus is Lord!

Studies in the Epistle to the Colossians
Chapter Six
THE ANALYSIS OF CHRISTIAN SERVICE

1. What is a "minister"? Does this definition describe your life for Christ?

2. Describe the *attitude* of ministry.

3. In Colossians 1:24, to whom does the "who" specifically refer?

4. Read Hebrews 12:1-4. Why should true ministering saints rejoice in "afflictions" and "sufferings" for the cause of Christ?
   A. Should a soldier expect to be bruised or wounded?
   B. According to II Timothy 3:12, should they expect persecution?

5. What is the *purpose* of ministering (Colossians 1:24; Ephesians 4:12 and 16)?

6. What is the *funnel* through which all ministries must to be directed and administrated?

7. Read Colossians 1:27. What was the result of "the riches of His glory among the Gentiles"?
   A. Why was this a "mystery" (Colossians 1:26)?
   B. To whom was it a "mystery"?

8. The *purpose* of evangelism is not to simply produce souls, but to produce _____.

9. What three statements in Colossians 1:28 relate the *methodology* of ministry?

10. According to Colossians 1:28, what is the intent of this methodology of ministry?

11. According to Colossians 1:29, what kind of effort does Christ expect of His servants?

12. Where will the energy come from for that kind of effort?

13. What will happen to people who try to put forth that kind of effort in their own strength?

Jesus is Lord!

Studies in the Epistle to the Colossians
Chapter Seven
THE ANALYSIS OF UNITY IN TRUTH

"[1] For I would that ye knew what great conflict I have for you, and for them at Laodicea, and for as many as have not seen my face in the flesh; [2] That their hearts might be comforted, being knit together in love, and unto all riches of the full assurance of understanding, to the acknowledgement of the mystery of God, and of the Father, and of Christ; [3] In whom are hid all the treasures of wisdom and knowledge. [4] And this I say, lest any man should beguile you with enticing words. [5] For though I be absent in the flesh, yet am I with you in the spirit, joying and beholding your order, and the stedfastness of your faith in Christ. [6] As ye have therefore received Christ Jesus the Lord, so walk ye in him: [7] Rooted and built up in him, and stablished in the faith, as ye have been taught, abounding therein with thanksgiving" (Colossians 2:1-7).

THE COMMUNITY IN UNITY (Colossians 2:1)

According to Colossians 2:1, the focus of the Lordship of Jesus is upon subjection to the truth of God's revealed will through His Word. That subjection should not be centrally motivated by a fear of chastisement, but by a love for Christ. The believer's love for Christ should motivate him to withstand the world's attacks, temptations, and persecutions.

Paul writes to a *corporation* of believers – a *community of faith* united by common beliefs and purposes. Jesus' Lordship over the corporate life of the church will only be seen as all of God's children are drawn together into a unity that centers itself in God's revealed truth - His Word. A unity in truth is a *unity of convictions* and that unity is an *unbreakable chain*.

According to Colossians 2:1, Paul wanted the Colossian church to "know" that he agonized (conflicted) in prayer for their unity in truth. Gnosticism was dividing the church both theologically and practically. Within Gnostic practices, the person with a *higher level* of *spiritual enlightenment* (knowledge) was naturally given more status within the church. This individual was exalted simply because some viewed him to be superior in intellect (knowledge of the depths of spiritual things). In most cases, this *knowledge* (Gnosis) resulted from his integration of pagan philosophies with biblical truth.

According to *Gnostic Scriptures and Fragments* (*Pistis Sophia: Book One*), Jesus gave the Apostles immediate knowledge of the twenty-four mysteries. In Gnosticism, the message of the Apostles was not the Gospel of Jesus Christ, which led people to faith in a Christ, regeneration, and discipleship. Salvation was leading people to *Gnosis* - the *knowledge* of these twenty-four ranks of mysteries. Once a person achieved this *knowledge*, he became part of the *Pleroma* (the divine realm of the gods and the ultimate Gnosis).

Paul's agonizing in prayer was not a struggle with God, but with the constant danger of the deception of these believers at Colosse and at Laodicea. Paul wanted them to know of his prayer life and his spiritual struggle on their behalf so that they might be encouraged to remain faithful and obedient to God's Word. God's encouragement is never just to make us feel good, but to motivate us to do that which we are encouraged to do. Therefore, biblical encouragement (exhortation) is intended to persuade us to perform the truth we own and to do what we claim to believe.

THE BOND OF UNITY IN TRUTH (Colossians 2:2)

There are two aspects of this unity in truth.

1. "Being knit together in love;" "A threefold cord is not quickly broken" (Ecclesiastes 4:12). This *threefold cord of unity* is:
   A. Love for one another
   B. Doctrinal foundations
   C. Submission to God's will

A primary means God uses to produce strength in a local church is a bond of love for one another. This refers to a partnership in ministry built upon the foundation of loving one another. This is contrary to *feeding* on each other by focusing on one another's weaknesses and failures. How can a church effectively love the lost if it cannot even love one another?

2. The knowledge "of full assurance of understanding," which is an accurate knowledge of God's Word, results in *sure convictions* (doctrinal foundations). This understanding will result in the *firm confidence* that Jesus is sovereign Lord.

The word "acknowledgement" in Colossians 2:2 is from the Greek word *epignosis* (ep-ig'-no-sis). It was a word used to describe full, perfect, experiential knowledge (as opposed to mere intellectual knowledge). The important thing to note here is that this complete knowledge (*epignosis*) came through the understanding of the Word of God, not through a host of intermediary luminaries. Peter speaks to this same issue in his epistle warning about the deception of Gnosticism.

"[1] Simon Peter, a servant and an apostle of Jesus Christ, to them that have obtained like precious faith with us through the righteousness of God and our Saviour Jesus Christ: [2] Grace and peace be multiplied unto you through the knowledge {*epignosis*} of God, and of Jesus our Lord, [3] According as his divine power hath given unto us all things that pertain unto life and godliness, through the knowledge {*epignosis*} of him that hath called us to glory and virtue: [4] Whereby are given unto us exceeding great and precious promises: that by these ye might be partakers of the divine nature, having escaped the corruption that is in the world through lust" (II Peter 1:1-4).

"[16] For we have not followed cunningly devised fables, when we made known unto you the power and coming of our Lord Jesus Christ, but were eyewitnesses of his majesty. [17] For he received from God the Father honour and glory, when there came such a voice to him from the excellent glory, This is my beloved Son, in whom I am well pleased. [18] And this voice which came from heaven we heard, when we were with him in the holy mount. [19] We have also a more sure word of prophecy; whereunto ye do well that ye take heed, as unto a light that shineth in a dark place, until the day dawn, and the day star arise in your hearts: [20] Knowing this first, that no prophecy of the scripture is of any private interpretation. [21] For the prophecy came not in old time by the will of man: but holy men of God spake as they were moved by the Holy Ghost" (II Peter 1:16-21).

The more completely a person understands God's Word, the firmer will be his resolve to see souls saved and to see lives changed. This mature believer will seek to give people an understanding of who God is and an understanding His expectations of His children. We do not gain knowledge of God only to possess knowledge. Real knowledge is converted to faith. Then real faith enables us to move forward in our service to God and our "work of the ministry." This generates spiritual confidence - not in ourselves or in our intellects, but in Christ who is revealed to us in His Word. This kind of confidence produces a stable foundation of knowledge and conviction that the earthquakes of cultural revolutions will never be able to move.

TWO FOUNDATIONS FOR UNITY IN TRUTH (Colossians 2:2-3)

1. Settled convictions are based upon a complete understanding of the "mystery of God, and of the Father, and of Christ (v. 2).

The "mystery" referred to in this verse is the *incarnational purpose* of God in Christ Jesus - God's complete propitiation and man's complete reconciliation and redemption (the Gospel message). The great truth of the incarnation is not that believers have found *truth*, but that *truth* has found them.

The "mystery" of the incarnation to the Gnostic mindset was unfathomable. This "mystery" involves the Theanthropic Christ. This term describes the uniqueness of

Jesus as God in human flesh - singular in being, yet with two distinct natures. The unity of a transcendent God with material beings was a complete contradiction to Gnostic beliefs.

The word "mysteries" is translated from the Greek word *musterion* (moos-tay'-ree-on). This word can have two meanings depending on your spiritual perspective. To the Gnostic, it meant *religious secrets*, confided only to the initiated at whatever level of illumination they had achieved. From a biblical perspective, "mysteries" means the *secret counsel* that governs God's dealings with the righteous, which are hidden from ungodly and wicked men but are plain to the godly.

2. Jesus is the source of all truth and wisdom (v. 3). There are no other intermediaries between God and men besides Jesus (I Timothy 2:5).

In Proverbs chapter eight, God speaks of His wisdom. He personalizes wisdom and equates it with Himself. He states that the person that finds wisdom, finds life (Proverbs 8:35). Is God talking about knowledge? He is and yet He is not! Yes, He is if that knowledge is knowledge of God and His ways. No, He is not if knowledge means attaining to and becoming the knowledge that God is. This latter is what Gnosticism believed.

The idea in Colossians 2:3 is that Christ is the *personification* of wisdom. The idea is that *all* wisdom is found in Jesus. There is no need to seek another source because He lacks nothing that needs to be known. To know who Christ is and what He has accomplished as the new Federal Head of the New Creation is to know and understand God's salvation. Faith simply receives that salvation as a gift from God. "In him {*Christ Jesus*} are hid all the treasures of wisdom and knowledge" (Colossians 2:3). "In Christ" all those treasures are fully and completely revealed to whosoever will.

THE PROTECTION OF UNITY IN TRUTH
False teachers are like wolves that steal and devour sheep. (Colossians 2:4-5)

"[27] For I have not shunned to declare unto you all the counsel of God. [28] Take heed therefore unto yourselves, and to all the flock, over the which the Holy Ghost hath made you overseers, to feed the church of God, which he hath purchased with his own blood. [29] For I know this, that after my departing shall grievous wolves enter in among you, not sparing the flock. [30] Also of your own selves shall men arise, speaking perverse things, to draw away disciples after them" (Acts 20:27-30).

The warning of Colossians 2:4 is against false teachers who offer something Jesus does not offer, or who ask you to do something Jesus does not ask you to do. The word "beguile" is from the Greek word *paralogizomai* (par-al-og-id'-zom-ahee). It means to cheat by false reckoning or deceive by false reasoning. The latter is the meaning in Colossians 2:4. "Enticing words" is the means of this deception. Spacious and seemingly intellectual discourses can be very persuasive. Be careful of human reasoning (any reasoning without Scriptural foundations).

People are often led astray by calculated, logical, and reasoned religious beliefs. If these religious beliefs are not Bible-based, they are without any foundation. Persuasive speech and logical discourse has imprisoned many people inside the gates of Hell.

In Colossians 2:5, Paul uses a military metaphor to describe unity in truth. The word "order" is from the Greek word *taxis* (tax'-is). Normally this was a military term denoting an orderly formation of soldiers. The structure of a local church (organization) is critical to protecting it against the infiltration of heresy. That is why God puts proven, spiritually mature leaders in administration of local churches (pastors and deacons). These individuals are God's front-line of offense against spiritual corruption.

The unity in truth that the Colossian church had was a strong front (based upon an exclusive loyalty to Christ) against attacks. When the arguments and attacks of deception came against the individual believers at Colosse, they took up battle stations to confront the error.

Unity in truth is a defense. We do not retreat under opposition, but stand our ground and fight regardless of the consequences (expect casualties). Evangelism is our offense. We must not only stand our ground, we must move forward to take more ground. This must be a collective and combined effort of all in a local church

The isolated Christian (existing outside of a doctrinally sound local church) is in constant danger of the gradual corrosive effects of a non-Christian culture. The degree of an individual's isolation from a biblically grounded body of believers will determine the degree of influence the world has upon on him. A *Lone Ranger Christian* is in constant danger of attack. The Lordship of Jesus Christ leads us into a close and deep relationship with God's community of faith.

THE CONFORMITY OF UNITY IN TRUTH
(Colossians 2:6-7)

"Received" in Colossians 2:6 is from the Greek word *paralambano* (par-al-am-ban'-o). It means to accept or acknowledge a person to be what he professes to be. In doing so, the approving party associates with the person he receives. This refers to the instruction of the Scriptures about the person of Jesus Christ that these believers had received from Paul. There are two basic pseudo-Scriptural approaches to the Lordship of Jesus.

1. Without careful analysis, the biblical demands of Jesus Christ become whatever a generation can determine Jesus to have been. Man creates God in his image. To one generation, He is a *revolutionary*. To another generation, He is a *magician* and *exorcist*. To our generation, He has been a great *social reformer*. In other words, each generation attempts to make Jesus what they are historically, rather than becoming what He is historically.

2. The second approach to the Lordship of Jesus is the central focus of experience related truths. In this case rightness, or correctness, is not determined by Scripture, but by experience. In other words, *this has happened to me, therefore this must be what Scripture means*. This is the determination of truth by experience, rather than the

evaluation of experience by truth. Experiences are often the greatest deceivers. Almost every cult is the by-product of a pseudo-religious experience (Mary Baker Eddy, Joseph Smith, etc.).

THE CONSISTENCY OF UNITY IN TRUTH
(Colossians 2:6)

There are two aspects of a biblical "walk . . . in" Christ (compare I Corinthians 15:58).

1. "Steadfastness" - the Christian walk is not a series of sprints, but steady forward progress.
2. "Unmovable" - loyalty to Christ means that nothing, or no one, should hold a higher place in our life than our loyalty to Jesus Christ.

THE BUILDING BLOCKS OF CONSISTENCY

The word "rooted" (Colossians 2:7) is from the Greek word *rhizoo* (hrid-zo'-o). It means to be once for all settled in a fixed spot, unmovable, fixed on truth, or firmly anchored in truth. "Built up in Him," (not *on*, but "in") refers to all that Jesus Christ is. This is the *environment* of our spiritual growth. His personality, His life, and His power should be our daily possession.

"Established in faith" - the more you try your faith, the more you proved God's ability to meet any and every need. The more that is done, the more established and stable our faith in God's abilities becomes.

"Abounding in thanksgiving" - stable faith in God's ability coincides with an abundance of thanksgiving. The transition is from questioning God's willingness to provide and supply to thanksgiving for His willingness to do so.

The centrality of biblical truth is the heart of unity. Christian unity is always *unity in truth*. Without truth, unity transcends to chaos and the disorder of instability. Without the stabilization of the absoluteness of God's Word, man will be little more than a piece of clay molded by the whims and fancies of the cultural and intellectual climate of a *bandwagon* Christianity.

Jesus is Lord!

Studies in the Epistle to the Colossians
Chapter Seven
THE ANALYSIS OF UNITY IN TRUTH

1. On what does the Lordship of Jesus focus the believer's attention?

2. What should be our central motivation for subjection to the Lordship of Jesus?

3. What made the local church at Colosse a *community in unity*?

4. According to Colossians 2:1, what did Paul want these believers to know he was doing on their behalf and why did he want them to know this?

5. In Colossians 2:2, Paul says these believers were "being knit together in love." What are the three elements of the threefold cord of unity?

6. What two things does a "full assurance of understanding" give to the believer?

7. How does false teaching destroy unity?

8. In Colossians 2:5, what is the military term Paul uses to describe unity in truth and what is the purpose in using this word?

9. Did God intend that any Christian ever exist in this world as a *lone wolf* without being accountable to a local assembly of believers?

10. List two false (pseudo) approaches to the Lordship of Jesus.

11. List two aspects of our "walk" (Colossians 2:6) from I Corinthians 15:58 necessary for consistency in unity in truth.

Jesus is Lord!

Studies in the Epistle to the Colossians
Chapter Eight
BIBLICAL WARNINGS

"Beware lest any man spoil you through philosophy and vain deceit, after the tradition of men, after the rudiments of the world, and not after Christ" (Colossians 2:8).

Ancient Gnosticism was a constantly fluid and evolving perversion of truth. It absorbed religious beliefs from most pagan religions as well as Judaism and Christianity. Both Judaism and Christianity were paganized by the corrupting philosophies of Gnosticism. This process of religious evolution is known as *Syncretism*. *Syncretism* is the combination of different beliefs or practices - the absorption and incorporation of various religious beliefs and practices. Ancient Gnosticism evolved into modern Gnosticism and is what we know today as Ecumenicism. It is about this process of *syncretism* that Paul warns in the epistle to the Colossians (as well as all local churches down through the ages).

The Colossian church was a local church surrounded by a society that mocked God, rejected authorities, experimented with Spiritism (Mysticism), and flirted with pagan cults. The historic period was also very materialistic enjoying all the material comforts of their time. It was this society's drawing power that was tempting the Colossian believers to abandon their distinctive Christian and biblical beliefs to become part of a larger and more socially acceptable community of people. To counteract this tendency, Paul confronts this local church at Colosse with one simple question - Is Jesus Lord?

Up to this point in the epistle, the Lordship of Jesus has been emphatically established. This brings the believer to a new question - is Jesus YOUR Lord? The attack against these Colossian believers (and all separated, Bible believing Christians) is a philosophical attack. When

75

believers accept human philosophies that are contradictory to the Word of God, they become the "spoil" of spiritual warfare. They then are taken captive by the enemy of Christ. These philosophies are an assault on the very foundation of Christianity (the Lordship of Jesus Christ).

COLOSSIANS 2:8 IS A WARNING.

For the church at Colosse, there were four elements of false teaching that posed a constant threat to these new believers and their local church.

1. The philosophies of men (vs. 8-15)
2. Jewish legalism (vs. 16-17)
3. Spiritism (Mysticism) (vs. 18-19) - these were spiritual mysteries revealed through spiritual mediums such as dead spirits or angels\demons.
4. Asceticism (vs. 20-23) - this involved a monastic lifestyle of self-denial, starvation, depravation of sleep, and self-flagellation.

These four elements continue to be a threat to individual Christians in various forms today. The continuing warning of the epistle is against all these individual heresies and their combined influence. Combined they created a very complex problem requiring solid theological foundations for spiritual discernment so as to avoid doctrinal contamination. The person contaminated with any one of these philosophies would become pre-occupied with its ridiculous teachings, which in turn would result in his uselessness for Christian service.

God's solution to the problem has been given in our previous study from Colossians 2:1-7. God wants believers to concentrate on laying solid doctrinal foundations based upon knowledge of Him and His Word. Doing this will unify believers in biblical truth.

SATAN'S COMMON TACTIC IS DIVIDING AND CONQUERING.

If he can split an army into small, fragmented groups, it is always easier to find a weakness. Satan then attacks at the weakest point. Within a local church, this is usually with new Christians who are not yet grounded in the Word of God. Or, it is in the lives of those who are not yet fully committed to the Lordship of Jesus Christ. This lack of commitment makes them continually vulnerable because they continue to live in the "flesh."

"For the flesh lusteth against the Spirit, and the Spirit against the flesh: and these are contrary the one to the other: so that ye cannot do the things that ye would" (Galatians 5:17).

ANALYZING THE WARNING - "BEWARE"

"Beware of false prophets, which come to you in sheep's clothing, but inwardly they are ravening wolves" (Matthew 7:15).

"Be sober, be vigilant; because your adversary the devil, as a roaring lion, walketh about, seeking whom he may devour" (I Peter 5:8).

The warnings in Matthew 7:15 and I Peter 5:8 are about accepting false teachers. The danger is being devoured by them. A fish that takes the bait is doomed to be devoured.

"Then Jesus said unto them, Take heed and beware of the leaven of the Pharisees and of the Sadducees" (Matthew 16:6).

The warning in Matthew 16:6 is against false doctrine ("leaven"). The danger is the prison that false doctrine creates in the practice of life. When God says "beware," He offers a warning that requires a constant vigilance on the believer's part in order to avoid corruption. The constant danger is that of being captured by false doctrines. When that happens, you become a traitor to the Lordship of Christ by joining the ranks of those propagating false doctrines.

THE MANNER OF CAPTURE ("SPOIL") IS THE PHILOSOPHIES OF MEN (FALSE DOCTRINES).

A philosophy is any system of thought or theory about the universe, its origins, man's purpose in it, and the meaning of life. A *biblical* philosophy answers all these questions by understanding the revelation about them from the Word of God. A *humanistic* philosophy answers these questions from man's own logic and reasoning outside of the Word of God (*exparte*). A philosophy can also be *humanistic* if it incorporates human logic or reasoning with revealed truth (example - *Theistic evolution*). God's Word exposes humanistic reasoning and logic to know Him, or the origins of existence, as completely unreliable.

> "[9] But as it is written, Eye hath not seen, nor ear heard, neither have entered into the heart of man, the things which God hath prepared for them that love him. [10] But God hath revealed them unto us by his Spirit: for the Spirit searcheth all things, yea, the deep things of God" (I Corinthians 2:9-10).

"Eye hath not seen, nor ear heard" - spiritual truth cannot be understood or discovered through *Empiricism*. *Empiricism* is the idea that truth can only be discovered by experience (the scientific method).

"Neither have entered into the heart of man" - spiritual things are totally incomprehensible to man's senses and it is impossible for lost men to fathom the reality of spiritual things. Science is *Empiricism*. Philosophy is *Rationalism*. Anything which is genuinely true scientifically or philosophically will also agree with Scriptural truth. Anything contradicting biblical truth, in whole, or in part is not true.

COLOSSIANS 2:8 - HUMAN PHILOSOPHIES ARE HOPELESS

Human philosophies are hopeless ("vain deceit") in their effort to help man with spiritual realities. They cannot give what they promise. For instance, a person who preaches salvation through human accomplishments ("works") cannot deliver on his promise. God is the only one capable of saving anyone and He will *only* do so by His own criteria.

"⁸ For by grace are ye saved through faith; and that not of yourselves: it is the gift of God: ⁹ Not of works, lest any man should boast" (Ephesians 2:8-9).

"Not by works of righteousness which we have done, but according to his mercy he saved us, by the washing of regeneration, and renewing of the Holy Ghost" (Titus 3:5).

To choose any one of the thousands of human philosophies of life (and their practices), that contradict the Word of God, is to be captured and carried away by Satan as a spoil of war. Is this warning being taken seriously by believers today? How many Christian parents (believing in an eternal Hell) would even think of risking the soul of their child by putting him in a Buddhist monastery, school of Islam, or a Roman Catholic school? Christians read the writings of all kinds of heretics because they are famous with little concern if they are true to God's Word. Radio preachers and television preachers bombard Christians with a buffet of heresy and few Christians have enough Bible knowledge to even know they have been taken as "spoil" by wolves in sheep clothing.

Many parents think nothing of putting their children into the hands of secular humanists, atheists, evolutionists, homosexuals, and hundreds of other philosophical perversions of truth each day in government run schools. These perversions of truth are complicated enough. Even a mature Christian would have difficulty dealing with these deceptions. How can we expect children to be able to survive in this environment? If Christians really took this warning seriously, there would be fewer evangelicals in bed with the harlot of Ecumenicism?

THE METHOD OF CAPTURE ("SPOIL") IS *INFILTRATION.*

The danger of corruption is increased because these philosophies often do not directly confront the believer. They sneak in under the guise of sincerity, devotion, and truth while they carry away the already weak and wounded to their den of deception. There are two main methods of deception resulting in capture:

1. "Traditions of men"

Simply because something is old and handed down through generations does not make it truth. As far as mankind is concerned, Satan's lies are almost as old as the revelation of God's truth to mankind. Tradition should not add one ounce of weight to anything. Old lies are no better than new lies. Almost all new philosophies are simply one man building on another man's outdated idea. They build by adding new error to the old error in order to modernize it and make it socially acceptable. There is nothing honorable or sacred about human traditions. They are little more than perpetuated ignorance.

> "The thing that hath been, it is that which shall be; and that which is done is that which shall be done: and there is no new thing under the sun" (Ecclesiastes 1:9).

> "[5] Then the Pharisees and scribes asked him, Why walk not thy disciples according to the tradition of the elders, but eat bread with unwashen hands? [6] He answered and said unto them, Well hath Esaias prophesied of you hypocrites, as it is written, This people honoureth me with their lips, but their heart is far from me. [7] Howbeit in vain do they worship me, teaching for doctrines the commandments of men. [8] For laying aside the commandment of God, ye hold the tradition of men, as the washing of pots and cups: and many other such like things ye do. [9] And he said unto them, Full well ye reject the commandment of God, that ye may keep your own tradition" (Mark 7:5-9).

2. "The rudiments of the world"

The word "rudiments" means elementary or infantile. Man's intellectual reasoning and rationalizations about the reality of God and existence compared to the revelation of God's Word are little more than a baby's *gah-gahs* or *coos*.

No matter how intellectual some of these philosophies appear, they are like the jungle native who offers sacrifice to the fire because it keeps him warm and cooks his food. "Rudiments" means to govern your life by infantile beliefs of mythology and human reasoning. We might compare this to getting a child to be good by lying to him about Santa Claus. Ceremonialism, sacramentalism, pagan symbolic mysteries, and initiatory rights are all rudimentary, infantile, and immature concepts based upon integrating humanistic philosophies and traditions with Christian beliefs. Legalism in any form is elementary and it is false religion.

"^{8} Howbeit then, when ye knew not God, ye did service unto them which by nature are no gods. ^{9} But now, after that ye have known God, or rather are known of God, how turn ye again to the weak and beggarly elements, whereunto ye desire again to be in bondage? ^{10} Ye observe days, and months, and times, and years. 11 I am afraid of you, lest I have bestowed upon you labour in vain" (Galatians 4:8-11).

"^{9} For in him dwelleth all the fulness of the Godhead bodily. ^{10} And ye are complete in him, which is the head of all principality and power" (Colossians 2:9-10).

Everything we need and want for understanding God, life, and the practice thereof is found in Jesus Christ. We need look nowhere else than to the revelation of the Word of God. Once you know the Jesus of the Word of God and His free gift of salvation, do not look elsewhere to know Him better. Search the Word more deeply to know Him more deeply.

"So then faith cometh by hearing, and hearing by the word of God" (Romans 10:17).

Many people who search for truth end up playing with rattles (human philosophies, intellectualism, and traditions of men) instead of laboring with the adult tools of God's Word to live a life of practical Christian service. Many of those rattles have a snake on the end of them.

"Neither let us tempt Christ, as some of them also tempted, and were destroyed of serpents" (I Corinthians 10:9).

Jesus is Lord!

Studies in the Epistle to the Colossians
Chapter Eight
BIBLICAL WARNINGS

1. What are the similarities between the culture of Colosse and ours that pose similar threats to believers of today?

2. According to Colossians 2:8, what is it that makes believers "spoils" of spiritual warfare?

3. What is the central statement for the foundation of the Christian faith to which these philosophies are an assault?

4. List the four elements of false teaching that pose a constant threat to believers and their local church.

5. From Colossians 2:1-7 and chapter seven, what is God's solution to this constant threat?

6. Specifically, about what is the "beware" warning of Colossians 2:8? What is the danger in failing to heed the warning?

7. What is a *philosophy*?

8. What does I Corinthians 2:9-10 reveal to us about man's abilities to know God, comprehend the source or our origins, or understand the forces behind our existence?

9. According to Colossians 2:8, what are the two methods that Satan will use to capture ("spoil") genuine believers?

10. What is a tradition?

11. What does the word "rudiment" mean as used in this context?

12. What is the only way of knowing if your belief system has been defiled and that you have been taken as spoil by these two things?

Jesus is Lord!

Studies in the Epistle to the Colossians
Chapter Nine
PROBLEMS AND SOLUTIONS

"[9] For in him dwelleth all the fulness of the Godhead bodily. [10] And ye are complete in him, which is the head of all principality and power" (Colossians 2:9-10).

At the time of the writing of the epistle to the Colossians, there were two basic syncretistic outlooks that prevailed in society. *(Syncretism is the social pressure on religions to compromise their distinctive beliefs in order to be in unity with the larger society.)* Jesus said, ". . . why call ye me, Lord, Lord, and do not the things which I say" (Luke 6:46)?

The two elements of syncretism (both remain in this philosophy today):

1. PRAGMATISM

Pragmatism is determining something's value based almost totally upon the practicality of its social application or the results produced. Therefore, a subjective definition of *success* becomes the measure of biblical correctness.

For instance, a central criticism of Fundamentalism by New-evangelicals is that Fundamentalism has failed to impact and change society. Their accusation against Fundamentalism is that it has lost its *cultural relevancy*. The reason Fundamentalism has failed to change society is because society continues to reject the biblical principles of Fundamentalism and because societies choose worldliness over holiness.

According to the philosophy of Pragmatism, something is determined to be impractical if it does not fit into a culture's accepted norms or social practices. Therefore, such things are rejected as impractical. Today this would apply to such things as modesty in dress, abstaining from alcoholic beverages, and premarital sex. Each of these things would be considered impractical in today's society and therefore rejected as binding moral principles.

2. ZEITGEIST

Zeitgeist is the *spirit of the age.* This defines the general intellectual, moral, and cultural climate of a historical era.

Zeitgeist refers to the moral and social influences of the trends, thoughts, and feelings of a society during a particular period of history. For instance, Jesus is often accepted and approved regarding salvation. In other words, it is socially acceptable to trust in Jesus for salvation and eternal life. However, His teachings are considered *out of date* and insufficient to meet man's needs for the everyday decisions and practices of life.

In this philosophy, the teachings of Jesus (the Word of God) could never solve the problems of individuals and their social predicaments. In this philosophy, Jesus has a minor part in a person's life. He certainly could not be described as being Lord of someone's life. If this is the case, then logic presumes that man must meet mankind's social needs while Jesus is sufficient only to meet man's limited spiritual needs. This is the *Zeitgeist* of the postmodern era.

HISTORICALLY, GNOSTICISM HAS ABSORBED AND INCORPORATED VARIOUS RELIGIOUS PHILOSOPHIES INTO ITS CULTUS.

This is a continuation of ancient Henotheism. Conquering nations absorbed the pagan idols (gods) of the conquered nation, adding that god to their pantheon of *gods.* This was pragmatic in that it generated the constantly evolving Zeitgeist (as it continues to do in modern times).

What has the philosophies of Pragmatism and Zeitgeist developed into within the Christian community?

1. Ritual observances were both invented and adopted from other religious practices (both Jewish and pagan).

2. Asceticism demanded abstinence in eating certain foods and anything someone might find pleasurable (even sexuality between a husband and wife). This developed into Monasticism.

3. Experience became the measurement of what was spiritually correct. For instance: a priest professes to receive the *baptism of the Spirit* while praying the *Rosary,* or a person is not completely *born again* until he has experienced *speaking in tongues.*

4. *Magic* and the *magician* were introduced into Christianity. *Magic* was introduced in the form of the mystical conference of grace through an ordained priest (*the magician*) as he administered some religious ritual (*sacrament*). This is purely of pagan origin. There is absolutely no biblical precedent for this idea.

THREE RESULTING PROBLEMS WERE CREATED FROM ALL OF THIS.

1. There is the problem of false religious knowledge (beliefs) that needs to be corrected. There were two main influences of false religious knowledge. Apostate Judaism contributed to legalistic traditionalism and ritualism (Matthew 23:1-8). Paganism contributed to mysticism (the conference of *grace,* which is really *magic,* from the gods through the priest to those who participate in some religious ritual or sacrifice).

2. There is the problem of people with false hopes of salvation. These *initiation rites* were common among mystical cults. A ritual washing (baptism) was common. When Israel began to adopt and incorporate pagan practices (Hellenization), circumcision was made into an initiatory rite. Circumcision was intended to be a physical ceremony that was an outward sign of the incorporation of an individual into the covenant of God with the nation of Israel. It identified that individual with the distinctive responsibilities of that covenant (especially separation from the licentious practices of heathenism). Under pagan influence (and later supported by the rationalism of Covenant Theology),

85

infant baptism replaced circumcision as an initiatory rite into Christianity.

3. There is the problem of false concepts of morality and ethics.

There was one solution offered to correct these three problems - the full acceptance of the Lordship of Jesus (Colossians 2:9-10).

The one solution to the problem of false religious beliefs is found in John 1:1-4 and 14. This solution returns individuals to *Sola Scriptura* (the Word of God alone) for the basis of faith (what to believe about God) and the practice of faith (God's instructions for life and practice).

"[1] In the beginning was the Word, and the Word was with God, and the Word was God. [2] The same was in the beginning with God. [3] All things were made by him; and without him was not any thing made that was made. [4] In him was life; and the life was the light of men" (John 1:1-4).

"And the Word was made flesh, and dwelt among us, (and we beheld his glory, the glory as of the only begotten of the Father,) full of grace and truth" (John 1:14).

Jesus is the *focal point* of all knowledge and truth. He is the *source* of all knowledge and truth. All knowledge and truth lead us to the Creator (Jesus Christ).

"[16] For by him were all things created, that are in heaven, and that are in earth, visible and invisible, whether they be thrones, or dominions, or principalities, or powers: all things were created by him, and for him: [17] And he is before all things, and by him all things consist" (Colossians1:16-17).

The one solution to the problem of people with false hope of salvation: Jesus is the only hope and means of salvation.

"[6] As ye have therefore received Christ Jesus the Lord, so walk ye in him: [7] Rooted and built up in him, and stablished in the faith, as ye have been taught, abounding therein with thanksgiving. [8] Beware lest any man spoil you through philosophy and vain deceit, after the tradition of men, after the rudiments of the world, and not after Christ. [9] For in him dwelleth all the fulness of the Godhead bodily. [10] And ye are complete in him, which is the head of all principality and power: [11] In whom also ye are circumcised with the circumcision made without hands, in putting off the body of the sins of the flesh by the circumcision of Christ: [12] Buried with him in baptism, wherein also ye are risen with him through the faith of the operation of God, who hath raised him from the dead" (Colossians 2:6-12).

"[4] And whither I go ye know, and the way ye know. [5] Thomas saith unto him, Lord, we know not whither thou goest; and how can we know the way? [6] Jesus saith unto him, I am the way, the truth, and the life: no man cometh unto the Father, but by me" (John 14:4-6).

"[8] Then Peter, filled with the Holy Ghost, said unto them, Ye rulers of the people, and elders of Israel, [9] If we this day be examined of the good deed done to the impotent man, by what means he is made whole; [10] Be it known unto you all, and to all the people of Israel, that by the name of Jesus Christ of Nazareth, whom ye crucified, whom God raised from the dead, even by him doth this man stand here before you whole. [11] This is the stone which was set at nought of you builders, which is become the head of the corner. [12] Neither is there salvation in any other: for there is none other name under heaven given among men, whereby we must be saved" (Acts 4:8-12).

"[1] Brethren, my heart's desire and prayer to God for Israel is, that they might be saved. [2] For I bear them record that they have a zeal of God, but not according to knowledge. [3] For they being ignorant of God's righteousness, and going about to establish their own righteousness, have not submitted themselves unto the righteousness of God. [4] For Christ is the end of the law for righteousness to every one that believeth" (Romans 10:1-4).

"[8] But what saith it? The word is nigh thee, even in thy mouth, and in thy heart: that is, the word of faith, which we preach; [9] That if thou shalt confess with thy mouth the Lord Jesus, and shalt believe in thine heart that God hath raised him from the dead, thou shalt be saved. [10] For with the heart man believeth unto righteousness; and with the mouth confession is made unto salvation. [11] For the scripture saith, Whosoever believeth on him shall not be ashamed. [12] For there is no difference between the Jew and the Greek: for the same Lord over all is rich unto all that call upon him. [13] For whosoever shall call upon the name of the Lord shall be saved" (Romans 10:8-13).

The one solution to the problem of false concepts of morality and ethics: study the Word of God.

"[14] Of these things put them in remembrance, charging them before the Lord that they strive not about words to no profit, but to the subverting of the hearers. [15] Study to shew thyself approved unto God, a workman that needeth not to be ashamed, rightly dividing the word of truth. [16] But shun profane and vain babblings: for they will increase unto more ungodliness" (II Timothy 2:14-16).

"[12] Yea, and all that will live godly in Christ Jesus shall suffer persecution. [13] But evil men and seducers shall wax worse and worse, deceiving, and being deceived. [14] But continue thou in the things which thou hast learned and hast been assured of, knowing of whom thou hast learned them; [15] And that from a child thou hast known the holy scriptures, which are able to make thee wise unto salvation through faith which is in Christ Jesus. [16] All scripture is given by inspiration of God, and is profitable for doctrine, for reproof, for correction, for instruction in righteousness: [17] That the man of God may be perfect, throughly furnished unto all good works" (II Timothy 3:12-17).

When Jesus is Lord (Colossians 2:10), He provides spiritual, moral, and mental completeness to the believer. His Word provides every answer to man's moral predicaments and search for truth. The majority of people who reject Jesus Christ and His gift of salvation do so because they know He has expectations for change in their lives once they become Christians. What they are really rejecting is the Lordship of Jesus over their lives. They want salvation, but they want to live after the manner of the world.

In rejecting the Lordship of Jesus over their lives, they accept the lordship of sin and Satan. In fear of being imprisoned by strict moral restraints, they become imprisoned to their own lusts. Through the lordship of sin, Satan destroys the lives of people.

When people say they want to be happy, it usually means they want *pleasure* (whatever it might cost). The price is usually borne by the people they use and abuse in their quest for that pleasure. Their pleasures become their prisons. Alcohol, other drugs, sex, and money all become the gods they worship and their prisons.

It all begins with one simple decision - rejecting the Lordship of Jesus Christ over their lives. That is not where it ends. It ends in pain and misery in the lives of everyone touched by this selfish pursuit after pleasure. This is where false religious beliefs always lead those it deceives. There is freedom in Jesus Christ from the prison of false hopes and addiction to sin.

"And ye shall know the truth and the truth shall make you free" (John 8:32).

"If the Son, therefore, shall make you free, ye shall be free indeed" (John 8:36).

Jesus is Lord!

Studies in the Epistle to the Colossians
Chapter Nine
PROBLEMS AND SOLUTIONS

1. Define Syncretism.

2. Give two elements of syncretism that influence today's society and define them.

3. List some of the practices into which the above two elements have developed within Christianity.

4. What are the three problems that result from all of this?

5. Give Scriptural evidence (references) why the full acceptance of the Lordship of Jesus is the one solution to each of these three problems.

6. What is the real reason behind people rejecting the Lordship of Jesus over their lives?

7. When people say they want to be happy, what does that usually mean in regard to the Lordship of Jesus?

8. When people want happiness (pleasure) at the sacrifice of holiness, have they rejected the Lordship of Jesus over their lives?

Jesus is Lord!

Studies in the Epistle to the Colossians
Chapter Ten
COMPLETELY COMPLETE

"[9] For in him dwelleth all the fulness of the Godhead bodily. [10] And ye are complete in him, which is the head of all principality and power: [11] In whom also ye are circumcised with the circumcision made without hands, in putting off the body of the sins of the flesh by the circumcision of Christ: [12] Buried with him in baptism, wherein also ye are risen with him through the faith of the operation of God, who hath raised him from the dead. [13] And you, being dead in your sins and the uncircumcision of your flesh, hath he quickened together with him, having forgiven you all trespasses; [14] Blotting out the handwriting of ordinances that was against us, which was contrary to us, and took it out of the way, nailing it to his cross; [15] And having spoiled principalities and powers, he made a shew of them openly, triumphing over them in it" (Colossians 2:9-15).

Gnosticism introduced the idea of *process salvation* into Christianity. Salvation became something *accomplished* or *achieved*, not something *received*. Salvation became a *series of steps* that one must go through or levels one must achieve. This made salvation, being "born again," a *process* rather than an *event*. This process involved various degrees of enlightenment with each step bringing a person closer to assurance of having achieved salvation (being part of the *Pleroma*). This process evolved into infant baptism, catechism, receiving Christ in the Eucharist, Church (denominational) membership, and keeping the commandments of God.

Salvation is not a process. Salvation is an instantaneous event in the life of a believer where he/she is immediately "born again" of the Spirit of God "by grace through faith" in the "finished" work of Christ Jesus. The majority of Christianity does not believe in completeness in

Christ Jesus. Any group that adds anything to who Christ is and what He has done, does not believe you can immediately be complete in Him. For instance, if you (or anyone) believe participation in any ritual, whether it is water baptism, circumcision, the Lord's Supper, or anything else, is necessary for your salvation then you also deny the completeness Christ offers. In this chapter we want to understand our completeness in Jesus Christ.

THE BASIS OF COMPLETENESS

> "When Jesus therefore had received the vinegar, he said, It is finished: and he bowed his head, and gave up the ghost" (John 19:30).

The last proclamation of Christ before His death on Calvary was that the work of redemption "is finished." All that He came to accomplish on man's behalf is complete. The most basic of human philosophies contradicting the Gospel is that which denies that the work of Christ for redemption is complete. If the work of Christ for redemption is not complete, mankind cannot have complete salvation. Any church, or person, that accepts this fallacy of the incompleteness of God's gift of salvation has committed the same blasphemy against God that Jeremiah warned Israel of in Jeremiah 2:1-13.

> "[1] Moreover the word of the LORD came to me, saying, [2] Go and cry in the ears of Jerusalem, saying, Thus saith the LORD; I remember thee, the kindness of thy youth, the love of thine espousals, when thou wentest after me in the wilderness, in a land that was not sown. [3] Israel was holiness unto the LORD, and the firstfruits of his increase: all that devour him shall offend; evil shall come upon them, saith the LORD. [4] Hear ye the word of the LORD, O house of Jacob, and all the families of the house of Israel: [5] Thus saith the LORD, What iniquity have your fathers found in me, that they are gone far from me, and have walked after vanity, and are become vain? [6] Neither said they, Where is the LORD that brought us up out of the land of Egypt, that led us through the wilderness, through a land of deserts and of pits, through a land of drought, and of the shadow of death, through a land that no man passed through, and where no man dwelt? [7] And I

brought you into a plentiful country, to eat the fruit thereof and the goodness thereof; but when ye entered, ye defiled my land, and made mine heritage an abomination. [8] The priests said not, Where is the LORD? and they that handle the law knew me not: the pastors also transgressed against me, and the prophets prophesied by Baal, and walked after things that do not profit. [9] Wherefore I will yet plead with you, saith the LORD, and with your children's children will I plead. [10] For pass over the isles of Chittim, and see; and send unto Kedar, and consider diligently, and see if there be such a thing. 11 Hath a nation changed their gods, which are yet no gods? but my people have changed their glory for that which doth not profit. [12] Be astonished, O ye heavens, at this, and be horribly afraid, be ye very desolate, saith the LORD. [13] For my people have committed two evils; they have forsaken me the fountain of living waters, and hewed them out cisterns, broken cisterns, that can hold no water" (Jeremiah 2:1-13).

Similarly to Jeremiah 2:13, Christians (true believers) have available to them a "fountain" that never fails in the finished work of Christ. Those who deny the completeness believers have in Christ, also create man-made sources for what they consider unfinished. This is a do it yourself salvation. Like the "broken cisterns" of Jeremiah 2:13, this false, misplaced faith will not hold water. What Christ has already "finished" is all anyone needs. He makes everything He touches whole. Let's see how.

THREE ASPECTS OF OUR COMPLETENESS IN CHRIST

1. Spiritual Circumcision and Spiritual Baptism - the first aspect of the "finished" work of Christ is complete salvation (Colossians 2:11-12). This is referred to as spiritual circumcision.

The influence of Judaism introduced the heresy that circumcision was necessary to complete salvation. They believed in a surgical salvation. Are you waiting to get certain sins removed from your life before you will become a believer or before you get saved? Christ says (Colossians 2:11) you have already been spiritually circumcised if you have trusted in the completeness He provides.

What is this true spiritual circumcision of which Paul speaks? It is the cutting away of the sin nature's power over our will. Spiritual circumcision is a spiritual surgery that only the work of the Cross could accomplish. Spiritual circumcision is the complete removal of the condemnation of the sin nature through the payment of the penalty (God's judgment) for sin and the satisfaction of God' justice (propitiation).

"[22] For I delight in the law of God after the inward man: [23] But I see another law in my members, warring against the law of my mind, and bringing me into captivity to the law of sin which is in my members. [24] O wretched man that I am! who shall deliver me from the body of this death? [25] I thank God through Jesus Christ our Lord. So then with the mind I myself serve the law of God; but with the flesh the law of sin. [1] There is therefore now no condemnation to them which are in Christ Jesus, who walk not after the flesh, but after the Spirit. [2] For the law of the Spirit of life in Christ Jesus hath made me free from the law of sin and death. [3] For what the law could not do, in that it was weak through the flesh, God sending his own Son in the likeness of sinful flesh, and for sin, condemned sin in the flesh: [4] That the righteousness of the law might be fulfilled in us, who walk not after the flesh, but after the Spirit" (Romans 7:22-8:4).

These verses separate between Saul (the old man) and Paul (the new nature). Sin is a synonym for his sin nature. As Romans 8:1 says, once a person puts trust in the finished work of Christ "there is now no condemnation" from God whatsoever, ever again.

Spiritual baptism is not water baptism. If Paul is dealing with a spiritual reality in circumcision, you can be sure He is dealing with the spiritual reality of baptism. Paul was combating traditionalistic ritualism. To make this baptism mean water is to contradict the whole argument he is presenting. Yet a baptism of some sort is accomplished by Christ in our salvation. What baptism is it? It is the baptism of the Holy Spirit!

The baptism of the Holy Spirit is the placement of each individual believer into the "body of Christ" (I

Corinthians 12:13). The word baptism means *placed into* or *immersed*. Water baptism is a physical picture of what takes place spiritually in our salvation.

> "³ Know ye not, that so many of us as were baptized into Jesus Christ were baptized into his death? ⁴ Therefore we are buried with him by baptism into death: that like as Christ was raised up from the dead by the glory of the Father, even so we also should walk in newness of life. ⁵ For if we have been planted together in the likeness of his death, we shall be also in the likeness of his resurrection: ⁶ Knowing this, that our old man is crucified with him, that the body of sin might be destroyed, that henceforth we should not serve sin" (Romans 6:3-6).

> "Buried with him in baptism, wherein also ye are risen with him through the faith of the operation of God, who hath raised him from the dead" (Colossians 2:12).

The instant a person puts faith in the "finished" work of Christ, that person is buried with Jesus in the sepulcher of Joseph of Arimathea two thousand years ago. Your faith positionally takes you back in time and hangs you on the cross with Jesus. That is the proclamation of faith. Your faith positionally puts you in the grave where you belong and He doesn't. That is the reality of faith. Yet, three days later, you receive something you don't deserve. You are positionally resurrected with Him. When Christ arose, you positionally rose with Him. That is what the reality of the baptism of the Spirit is all about. It is your placement into the body of Christ. All that His body experienced physically, we positionally experience spiritually.

How is this accomplished? It is an act of God (Colossians 2:12). "Operation" is from the Greek word *energeia* (en-erg'-i-ah). It means energy. However, the word is always is used to refer to superhuman power in the New Testament. This act of God is procured by "faith."

> "That if thou shalt confess with thy mouth the Lord Jesus, and shalt believe in thine heart that God hath raised him from the dead, thou shalt be saved" (Romans 10:9).

Now pay close attention, this is extremely important that you understand! You see, a miracle took place in God's "operation" when you were buried with Christ. That "old man" was buried also. He died (Romans 6:6). He was positionally crucified and buried with Christ. That "old man" was the one condemned to an eternal hell. In the miracle of Christ's resurrection ("the operation of God"), the believer is positionally and eternally separated from that "old man." The "old man" was positionally left in the grave and the believer was set free.

2. Our completeness in Christ is the complete remission of the sin penalty (Colossians 2:13-14).

In complete salvation the emphasis is *completeness apart from ritual.* In the complete remission of sin the emphasis is *complete righteousness apart from human participation* and the complete removal of any sin that might condemn us through the payment of its penalty. As a result the believer is "made alive."

Before trusting Christ the believer was "dead in your sins." Without Christ, everyone is helplessly condemned and on death row awaiting execution of capital punishment. Before trusting Christ the believer was "dead in your uncircumcision of your flesh." This means he is totally corrupted and under the power of the "old man" with no continuing power over the fallen nature.

In Colossians 2:14a, the word "handwriting" is a word that refers to a self-confessed recognition of a debt owed. It is translated from the Greek word *cheirographon* (khi-rog'-raf-on). It refers to a *written confession.* Essentially this makes the death, burial, and resurrection of Christ the believer's *spiritual eraser.* Jesus nailed that confession to the Cross and marked it *Paid in Full.* The debt was removed.

3. Our completeness in Christ is complete victory (Colossians 2:15).

"[14] Forasmuch then as the children are partakers of flesh and blood, he also himself likewise took part of the same; that through death he might destroy him that had the power of death, that is, the devil; [15] And deliver them who through fear of death were all their lifetime subject to bondage" (Hebrews 2:14-15).

Satan's dominion (God's curse upon sin) over our fallen nature was broken and destroyed at Calvary. The victory over death provided by Christ's substitutionary death, burial, and resurrection is the believer's present possession.

"[54] So when this corruptible shall have put on incorruption, and this mortal shall have put on immortality, then shall be brought to pass the saying that is written, Death is swallowed up in victory. [55] O death, where is thy sting? O grave, where is thy victory? [56] The sting of death is sin; and the strength of sin is the law. [57] But thanks be to God, which giveth us the victory through our Lord Jesus Christ" (I Corinthians 15:54-57).

Do you know this completeness today? Is your salvation a complete salvation? Does your salvation recognize the complete remission of the sin penalty and all the guilt and anguish that goes with it? If that is not your salvation, you don't have the salvation that Christ gives as a free gift received by faith.

Are you living in the sure knowledge of a complete and already accomplished victory, or are you still living under Satan's dominion? There is no need to live there! His power was broken two thousand years ago. The victor's claim to victory is found in the words - "greater is He that is in you than he that is in the world." Claim your completeness in Christ Jesus today and live in that completeness.

Jesus is Lord!

Studies in the Epistle to the Colossians
Chapter Ten
COMPLETELY COMPLETE

1. Define *process salvation*.

2. The majority of that which calls itself Christianity does not believe in a completed work of salvation. What do they do to complete the salvation they see as incomplete?

3. What is the significance of the cry of the Cross recorded in John 19:30 as these few words describe the work of redemption that Christ came to accomplish?

4. Read Jeremiah 2:1-13. From verse 13, what do all true believers have available to them in the finished work of Christ?

5. List the three aspects of a complete salvation.

6. What is the spiritual circumcision that Paul refers to in Colossians 2:11-12 as opposed to the *surgical salvation* introduced into Christianity by apostate Judaism? If water baptism is the means by which a person's salvation is completed, isn't that the same type of thing (*bathtub salvation*)?

7. Discuss spiritual baptism. What is it (give Scripture)?

8. How does Romans 8:1 confirm a completed gift of salvation?

9. Read Colossians 3:12. How can a believer living in the 20th century be "buried" with Christ?
    A. How can a person be living and yet be "risen" with Christ?
    B. How is this accomplished?
    C. How is it procured?

10. In Colossians 2:14, how does the word "handwriting" relate to us and what is the significance of it being nailed to the Cross?

11. Read Hebrews 2:14-15 and I Corinthians 15:54-57 and make some Scriptural conclusions about Satan's dominion and our victory in Christ's finished work for salvation.

Jesus is Lord!

Studies in the Epistle to the Colossians
Chapter Eleven
THE DEVASTATING INFLUENCES
OF FALSE DOCTRINE

"[16] Let no man therefore judge you in meat, or in drink, or in respect of an holyday, or of the new moon, or of the sabbath days: [17] Which are a shadow of things to come; but the body is of Christ. [18] Let no man beguile you of your reward in a voluntary humility and worshipping of angels, intruding into those things which he hath not seen, vainly puffed up by his fleshly mind, [19] And not holding the Head, from which all the body by joints and bands having nourishment ministered, and knit together, increaseth with the increase of God. [20] Wherefore if ye be dead with Christ from the rudiments of the world, why, as though living in the world, are ye subject to ordinances, [21] (Touch not; taste not; handle not; [22] Which all are to perish with the using;) after the commandments and doctrines of men? [23] Which things have indeed a shew of wisdom in will worship, and humility, and neglecting of the body; not in any honour to the satisfying of the flesh" (Colossians 2:16-23).

Having already established the true believer's freedom from the prison of dead ritualism and futile attempts at self-righteousness, Paul goes on to caution against being influenced and intimidated into false ethical practices by three unscriptural belief systems.

Ethics are a derivative of our belief system (doctrine). **Ethics are moral rules that govern our actions involving a response to certain situations of life.** These may include responses to certain temptations to sin or personal responsibilities that need to be fulfilled. When our doctrine is correct, the ethical rules governing our lives will be correct.

Paul is dealing with three areas of false teaching that establish false moral ethics. These false moral ethics bring restraints that are extra-Biblical. They involve the believer in things that are empty of any spiritual value.

These three false teachings are legalism, mysticism, and asceticism. All three of these false teachings involve the professing believer in practices that deny his completeness in Christ. Each of these false teachings integrated pagan beliefs and human philosophies with biblical truth. Any one of these false teachings is extremely dangerous and deadly to a real faith in Christ.

LEGALISM - COLOSSIANS 2:14-16 -

Legalism found its beginnings in the mixture of apostate Judaism and Gnosticism. The warning of Colossians 2:16 is against being pressured ("judge you") into the false religious practices that are listed. These things were part of the Old Covenant and were only intended to provide *types*. These *types* were fulfilled in the New Covenant in the life, death, and resurrection of Jesus Christ. They were only *shadows* (v. 17) of that which Christ and His finished work are the reality. The believer's completeness (Colossians 2:10) lies in what Christ has already accomplished.

> "[1] O foolish Galatians, who hath bewitched you, that ye should not obey the truth, before whose eyes Jesus Christ hath been evidently set forth, crucified among you? [2] This only would I learn of you, Received ye the Spirit by the works of the law, or by the hearing of faith? [3] Are ye so foolish? having begun in the Spirit, are ye now made perfect by the flesh? [4] Have ye suffered so many things in vain? if it be yet in vain. [5] He therefore that ministereth to you the Spirit, and worketh miracles among you, doeth he it by the works of the law, or by the hearing of faith? [6] Even as Abraham believed God, and it was accounted to him for righteousness. [7] Know ye therefore that they which are of faith, the same are the children of Abraham. [8] And the scripture, foreseeing that God would justify the heathen through faith, preached before the gospel unto Abraham, saying, In thee shall all nations be blessed. [9] So then they which be of faith are blessed with faithful Abraham. [10] For as many as are of the works of the law are under the curse: for it is written, Cursed is every one that

100

continueth not in all things which are written in the book of the law to do them. [11] But that no man is justified by the law in the sight of God, it is evident: for, The just shall live by faith" (Galatians 3:1-11).

Completeness ("perfect," v. 3) does not come through religious ritual, ceremony, or obeying laws. If a person's participation in religious rituals or ceremonies could make him right with God, what was the purpose of Christ's incarnation, death, and resurrection?

"[28] He that despised Moses' law died without mercy under two or three witnesses: [29] Of how much sorer punishment, suppose ye, shall he be thought worthy, who hath trodden under foot the Son of God, and hath counted the blood of the covenant, wherewith he was sanctified, an unholy thing, and hath done despite unto the Spirit of grace? [30] For we know him that hath said, Vengeance belongeth unto me, I will recompense, saith the Lord. And again, The Lord shall judge his people. [31] It is a fearful thing to fall into the hands of the living God" (Hebrews. 10:28-31).

Trusting in anything other than a finished work of redemption in the blood of Christ is a denial of the finished work of Christ. Such false faith is also an insult against the grace of God. The *theory-ology* of legalism said Christ died for our sins, but the believer stills needs to eat the foods ordained in the Old Covenant, keep certain holy days, be circumcised, and offer the necessary sacrifices in order to be right with God. Many early Christians (especially Jewish believers) were deceived into believing this. This deception resulted in misplaced faith. This misplaced faith kept them from true faith and truly being saved ("born again').

"[1] Brethren, my heart's desire and prayer to God for Israel is, that they might be saved. [2] For I bear them record that they have a zeal of God, but not according to knowledge. [3] For they being ignorant of God's righteousness, and going about to establish their own righteousness, have not submitted themselves unto the righteousness of God. [4] For

Christ is the end of the law for righteousness to every one that believeth" (Romans 10:1-4).

The day of the "new moon" referred to in Colossians 2:16 was placed alongside the Sabbath as a day of importance. Special messengers were established to watch for the exact time of its beginning. Originally, the intended purpose was to remind Old Covenant believers to diligently watch for the coming of Messiah to establish His Kingdom on earth. This purpose was completely lost in misunderstanding. Therefore, its purpose in faith was lost and faith was misplaced.

"[1] Thus saith the Lord GOD; The gate of the inner court that looketh toward the east shall be shut the six working days; but on the sabbath it shall be opened, and in the day of the new moon it shall be opened. [2] And the prince shall enter by the way of the porch of that gate without, and shall stand by the post of the gate, and the priests shall prepare his burnt offering and his peace offerings, and he shall worship at the threshold of the gate: then he shall go forth; but the gate shall not be shut until the evening. [3] Likewise the people of the land shall worship at the door of this gate before the LORD in the sabbaths and in the new moons" (Ezekiel 46:1-3; compare I Kings 8:14, 22; II Kings 11:14, 23:3).

"Sabbaths" were weekly Sabbath days. These Sabbath days had also come to mean the exact opposite of what God intended them to mean.

"[12] And the LORD spake unto Moses, saying, [13] Speak thou also unto the children of Israel, saying, Verily my sabbaths ye shall keep: for it is a sign between me and you throughout your generations; that ye may know that I am the LORD that doth sanctify you. [14] Ye shall keep the sabbath therefore; for it is holy unto you: every one that defileth it shall surely be put to death: for whosoever doeth any work therein, that soul shall be cut off from among his people. [15] Six days may work be done; but in the seventh is the sabbath of rest, holy to the LORD: whosoever doeth any work in the sabbath day, he shall surely be put to death. [16] Wherefore the children of Israel shall keep the sabbath, to observe the sabbath throughout

102

their generations, for a perpetual covenant. [17] It is a sign between me and the children of Israel for ever: for in six days the LORD made heaven and earth, and on the seventh day he rested, and was refreshed" (Exodus 31:12-17).

Working on a Sabbath day signified, in a physical way, that an individual had not entered into God's provided rest. This physical rest was a "shadow" of a believer's completeness, which would be provided in the substitutionary work of Messiah. Working on the Sabbath manifested an inadequate faith that brought a death sentence upon that person. The leaders of the Old Covenant had come to teach that keeping the Sabbath was part of the *process of salvation* (keeping the Law), which was a complete misrepresentation of its purpose.

All of these Old Covenant practices were just types that were fulfilled in the finished work of Christ. They were *shadows* of that future reality. When you see a shadow there must be a body of substance that casts it. Christ and His finished work at Calvary are the "body" (Colossians 2:17). The "body" refers to the believer's completeness in the reality of Christ's finished work of redemption.

The warning against legalism is about being careful not to confuse the *shadows* with the "body." Do not rely on the shadows (religious rituals and ceremonies) for your completeness. The *shadows* cannot provide completeness. Any religious practice that does not testify to our completeness in Christ, denies that completeness. To accept the "shadow" over the reality is to reject the reality for the "shadow."

If your completeness is not based solely upon the finished work of Christ offered as a free gift of grace and received by simple, but absolute faith, it is not biblical completeness. In that case, your Christianity is not biblical Christianity.

"[1] Stand fast therefore in the liberty wherewith Christ hath made us free, and be not entangled again with the yoke of bondage. [2] Behold, I Paul say unto you, that if ye be circumcised, Christ shall profit you nothing. ³ For I testify again to every man that is circumcised, that he is a debtor to do the whole law. ⁴ Christ is become of no effect unto you, whosoever of you are justified by the law; ye are fallen from grace. ⁵ For we through the Spirit wait for the hope of righteousness by faith. ⁶ For in Jesus Christ neither circumcision availeth any thing, nor uncircumcision; but faith which worketh by love. ⁷ Ye did run well; who did hinder you that ye should not obey the truth? ⁸ This persuasion cometh not of him that calleth you. 9 A little leaven leaveneth the whole lump" (Galatians 5:1-9).

Trust in any religious ritual, ceremony, or any attempt at self-righteousness for completeness before God is evidence that faith is not in Christ for that completeness. Instead, faith is in religious "works of righteousness." Just a "little" (any) of that misplaced faith "leaveneth the whole" of that person's faith. In other words, the whole of that person's faith is equal to no faith at all.

Mysticism and Asceticism will be dealt with in the next chapter.

Jesus is Lord!

Studies in the Epistle to the Colossians

Chapter Eleven

THE DEVASTATING INFLUENCES OF FALSE DOCTRINE

1. What are ethics (moral rules governing actions and responsibilities) based upon?

2. What are the three areas of false teaching that Paul warns about in Colossians 2:14-23?

3. What is the result of the acceptance of any of these false teachings in contrast to Paul's teaching that the believer is "complete" in Christ?

4. In Colossians 2:16, what does "let no man therefore judge you" mean?

5. What is meant that the things listed in Colossians 2:16 were only "a shadow of things to come"? What causes the existence of a shadow?

6. What does the word "body" in Colossians 2:17 refer to theologically (compare verse 10)? What is the basis of the believer's completeness in Christ?

7. Read Galatians 3:1-3. According to these verses, what cannot provide completeness?

8. If a person's participation in religious rituals or ceremonies could make him right with God, what was the purpose of Christ's incarnation, death and resurrection?

9. Read Hebrews 10:29. From your understanding of this verse, what will be the outcome of accepting the false teaching about any one of the practices listed in Colossians 3:16?

10. Read Ezekiel 46:1-4. What was the original intended purpose of watching and observing the days of the "new moon"?

11. Read Exodus 31:12-17. What was the original purpose of keeping the Sabbath and why was a death sentence upon those who failed to do so?

12. Read Galatians 5:1-9. What does trust in any form of religious ritual or practice say about our completeness in the work of Christ?

Jesus is Lord!

Studies in the Epistle to the Colossians

Chapter Twelve

LET NO MAN BEGUILE YOU

"[18] Let no man beguile you of your reward in a voluntary humility and worshipping of angels, intruding into those things which he hath not seen, vainly puffed up by his fleshly mind, [19] And not holding the Head, from which all the body by joints and bands having nourishment ministered, and knit together, increaseth with the increase of God" (Colossians 2:18-19).

Very often people do not even consider the ramifications of false doctrine upon a life. False doctrine leads to false practices. False practices lead to lives wasted in increments of time spent on nonsensical religious endeavors. Religion is man pursuing God through philosophies and human traditions. Christianity is God pursuing people through love, mercy, grace, and truth. The Christian must be cautious he is not beguiled into false religious practices that eat up his life in small bites of wasted pursuits. We must be careful to never mistake religious zeal for orthodoxy.

"[1] Brethren, my heart's desire and prayer to God for Israel is, that they might be saved. [2] For I bear them record that they have a zeal of God, but not according to knowledge. [3] For they being ignorant of God's righteousness, and going about to establish their own righteousness, have not submitted themselves unto the righteousness of God" (Romans 10:1-3).

The proper presentation of the Gospel leads a person to both an understanding of his completeness in the finished work of redemption and the sovereign right of Jesus to be the Lord of those He redeems. He is the "Head" of the "body" that is formed by individuals trusting in the completeness He provides in the gift of salvation.

The whole of the epistle to the Romans leads to a

pinnacle for the reception of Christ as Lord. Paul is condemning certain religious practices that contradict believer's completeness in Jesus Christ. "And ye are complete in him, which is the head of all principality and power" (Colossians 2:10). Therefore, these contradicting practices against the believer's completeness in Jesus Christ are a denial of Jesus' right to absolute Lordship over the believer's life. Although these practices are seemingly innocent and harmless, they were actually serious deviations that severed the Lordship of Jesus Christ from believers. The metaphor is that these false practices sever the Head from the body.

As stated in the last chapter, these three false practices are legalism, mysticism, and asceticism. Each of these three false practices is a false presentation of an alternative acceptable road to completeness and access to God. Legalism was dealt with in the last chapter. Mysticism and asceticism will be dealt with in this chapter.

WHAT IS MYSTICISM?

Mysticism is praying to *angels* or communicating with *spirits* as mediators and intercessors between God and men. Mysticism came from the influence of the pagan mystery religions. Mysticism often involved miraculous visions and spirits speaking through people (this was the common pagan practice of "tongues"). The false teacher of Mysticism involved those he had "beguiled" into seeking various experiences through contact with *spiritual messengers* ("angels") capable of communicating with God (*the gods in pagan religions*).

If Satan can get a person to be dependent upon anyone other than Jesus Christ, he has succeeded in creating another mediator and intercessor that replaces Jesus Christ in that person's life. One of Satan's greatest deceptions to accomplish this is to get the professing believer to focus on his own religious experiences and to begin seeking after miracles in his life. That person thinks he is involved in worshipping God. Actually he is "voluntarily" submitting himself to *spiritual beings* (fallen angels or demons) and is worshipping those *spiritual beings* by seeking religious experiences and miracles through them.

Other than God, the only spiritual beings that exist are "angels." They exist as demon's (fallen angels) and a heavenly host of holy angels. Although angels can do marvelous works, they do so only by the authority of God and by His permission and delegation.

WHY DOES GOD CONDEMN SEEKING ANGELS TO BRING ABOUT MIRACLES, VISIONS, OR RELIGIOUS EXPERIENCES?

God is the source of these things. Nowhere in Scripture is man directed to seek after these things. Angels were created to minister to mankind, not to be worshipped by mankind. Humans are naturally awed by things beyond their comprehension. This awe makes people susceptible to worshipping things and beings that should not be worshipped.

Worship is giving worth to something. If we see a wonderful peace of craftsmanship, we would not think of praising the tools involved in its production. Our attention would be given to the craftsman who used the tools. If we see a beautiful painting, we would not think to praise the canvas or paint brushes involved in its production. We would praise the artist whose talent created the painting. If our ears are blessed with the music of a master, we would not praise the instrument he played. Our attention would be drawn to the skillful musician in the use of the instrument. Angels are simply God's instruments as He works His masterpiece of love in the redemption of souls.

"Are they not all ministering spirits, sent forth to minister for them who shall be heirs of salvation" (Hebrews 1:14)?

God's heavenly hosts of holy angels do not want man's worship. In fact, anytime worship was given to one of them, they immediately stopped it and redirected that worship to God. Any kind of preoccupation with angels is a form of false worship coming from false doctrine.

"[15] Take ye therefore good heed unto yourselves; for ye saw no manner of similitude on the day *that* the LORD spake unto you in Horeb out of the midst of the fire: [16] Lest ye corrupt *yourselves*, and make you a graven image, the similitude of any figure, the likeness of male or female, [17] The likeness of any beast that *is* on the earth, the likeness of any winged fowl that flieth in the air, [18] The likeness of any thing that creepeth on the ground, the likeness of any fish that *is* in the waters beneath the earth: [19] And lest thou lift up thine eyes unto heaven, and when thou seest the sun, and the moon, and the stars, *even* all the host of heaven, shouldest be driven to worship them, and serve them, which the LORD thy God hath divided unto all nations under the whole heaven" (Deuteronomy 4: 15-19).

"[5] And a voice came out of the throne, saying, Praise our God, all ye his servants, and ye that fear him, both small and great. [6] And I heard as it were the voice of a great multitude, and as the voice of many waters, and as the voice of mighty thunderings, saying, Alleluia: for the Lord God omnipotent reigneth. [7] Let us be glad and rejoice, and give honour to him: for the marriage of the Lamb is come, and his wife hath made herself ready. [8] And to her was granted that she should be arrayed in fine linen, clean and white: for the fine linen is the righteousness of saints. [9] And he saith unto me, Write, Blessed *are* they which are called unto the marriage supper of the Lamb. And he saith unto me, These are the true sayings of God. [10] And I fell at his feet to worship him. And he said unto me, See *thou do it* not: I am thy fellowservant, and of thy brethren that have the testimony of Jesus: worship God: for the testimony of Jesus is the spirit of prophecy" (Revelation 19:5-10).

"[8] And I John saw these things, and heard *them*. And when I had heard and seen, I fell down to worship before the feet of the angel which shewed me these things. [9] Then saith he unto me, See *thou do it* not: for I am thy fellowservant, and of thy brethren the prophets, and of them which keep the sayings of this book: worship God" (Revelation 22:8-9).

Satan and all fallen angels want the worship of mankind.

"And saith unto him, All these things will I give thee, if thou wilt fall down and worship me" (Matthew 4:9).

"[12] How art thou fallen from heaven, O Lucifer, son of the morning! how art thou cut down to the ground, which didst weaken the nations! [13] For thou hast said in thine heart, I will ascend into heaven, I will exalt my throne above the stars of God: I will sit also upon the mount of the congregation, in the sides of the north: [14] I will ascend above the heights of the clouds; I will be like the most High. [15] Yet thou shalt be brought down to hell, to the sides of the pit" (Isaiah 14:12-15).

"[8] Again, the devil taketh him up into an exceeding high mountain, and sheweth him all the kingdoms of the world, and the glory of them; [9] And saith unto him, All these things will I give thee, if thou wilt fall down and worship me. [10] Then saith Jesus unto him, Get thee hence, Satan: for it is written, Thou shalt worship the Lord thy God, and him only shalt thou serve" (Matthew 4:8-10).

The worship of, or dependence on, any spiritual being other than God is Satanic in origin. Satan wants to get you off track by getting you to chase after some religious experience or some higher plane of knowledge. If he succeeds, he will keep you from focusing your efforts on growing in the knowledge of the Lord. He will keep you from growing in spiritual maturity and from ministering to others. There is only one mediator between God and men.

"For there is one God, and one mediator between God and men, the man Christ Jesus" (I Timothy 2:5).

According to Colossians 2:18, any person claiming he is guided by a new revelation, an extra-biblical vision, or from direct extra-biblical communication from God is a mystic (another word for this person is a Medium). Paul says this person is "intruding into those things which he hath not seen." In other words, he is involving himself with spiritual beings and things with which he has no business. He is "intruding" into an area that is forbidden because he is "vainly puffed up" by his own carnal mind. That person is really chasing after recognition and vain glory for a spiritual connection that gives him spiritual superiority (status).

WHAT HAPPENS WHEN WE ALLOW JESUS TO GOVERN OUR LIVES THROUGH THE WORD OF GOD (COLOSSIANS 2:19)?

The illustration of Colossians 2:19 is that each part of the *body* will only function properly when the right *head* is in control. Legalism, Mysticism, and Asceticism are false doctrines that lead us in false directions. They involve us in worthless and empty pursuits that benefit no one. The message of Colossians 2:19 is that the proper exercise of the human will can only be achieved by accepting the correct leadership, direction, and communication from the correct Lord. The Lord Jesus directs people to do His will through His Word (II Timothy 3:16-17). The source of all spiritual "nourishment" (*for growth*) is the Lordship of Jesus Christ and His inspired Words inscripturalized in the sixty-six books of the Bible.

WHAT IS ASCETICISM?

Asceticism is the religion of false worship through human regulations. It is spiritual legalism. Asceticism puts extreme unbiblical and extra-biblical restraints and expectations upon people. Only those practicing extreme forms of self-denial could be truly considered *spiritual* (there are many degrees of this). Asceticism is the outgrowth of Dualism and is based upon the false belief that all material matter was evil. The spiritual could have no contact with the material. Therefore, the more a person was able to restrain himself from participation in the physical *(especially things that brought pleasure such as marriage, food, sleep, comfort, etc.),* the closer he would be to God. Monasticism developed from this false philosophy. Asceticism is summed up by the words "Touch not; taste not; handle not" (Colossians 2:21). The believer's completeness in Christ gives him perfect and immediate access to God.

"Let us therefore come boldly unto the throne of grace, that we may obtain mercy, and find grace to help in time of need" (Hebrews 4:16).

The believer's completeness in Christ opened the door for intimate fellowship with God.

"That which we have seen and heard declare we unto you, that ye also may have fellowship with us: and truly our fellowship is with the Father, and with his Son Jesus Christ" (I John 1:3).

"[6] If we say that we have fellowship with him, and walk in darkness, we lie, and do not the truth: [7] But if we walk in the light, as he is in the light, we have fellowship one with another, and the blood of Jesus Christ his Son cleanseth us from all sin" (I John 1:6-7).

Nothing needs to be added to what Christ has already done.

1. Legalism adds nothing to what Christ has done. In fact it denies what He has done and is doing in our lives.
2. Mysticism denies the intermediary work of Christ and establishes such beings as angels, dead saints, and the virgin Mary as intercessors between God and man.
3. Asceticism denies the believer's spiritual union in Christ. Since its philosophical foundation believes there can be no contact between the spiritual and material, it also denies the baptism and indwelling of the Holy Spirit.

All three of these false doctrines deny the believer's completeness in Christ. To accept anyone of these philosophies is to be "spoiled" as a Christian; "beware!"

Jesus is Lord!

Studies in the Epistle to the Colossians
Chapter Twelve
LET NO MAN BEGUILE YOU

1. What two things does the proper presentation of the Gospel lead us to understand?

2. Read Romans 10:1-13. To what is the pinnacle that the previous teaching of the book of Romans leads us?

3. What is the contradiction of this that Paul is condemning in Colossians 2:16-23?

4. What do the three false teachings of Colossians 2:16-19 do in their relationship to the Lordship of Jesus Christ?

5. What is Mysticism?

6. What is the name given to the spiritual messengers by the Mystics who had incorporated their pagan beliefs into Christianity?

7. Does God ever tell believers to communicate to Him through angels?

8. What spiritual beings exist in the spiritual realm? What are the fallen beings called?

9. Give some of the reasons why God condemns seeking angels to bring about miracles, answer prayer, or give visions or religious experiences.

10. According to Isaiah 14:12-15 and Matthew 4:8-10, what do fallen angels want from mankind? According to Hebrews 1:14, what is God's intended order?

11. Define Asceticism and the central false belief behind this false philosophy.

Jesus is Lord!

Studies in the Epistle to the Colossians

Chapter Thirteen
SET YOUR AFFECTION ON THINGS ABOVE

"[1] If ye then be risen with Christ, seek those things which are above, where Christ sitteth on the right hand of God. [2] Set your affection on things above, not on things on the earth. [3] For ye are dead, and your life is hid with Christ in God. [4] When Christ, who is our life, shall appear, then shall ye also appear with him in glory" (Colossians 3:1-4).

As we move deeper into Colossians, we need to see the order of teaching of the truth by the Spirit of God. Paul now begins to lay out some practical applications of truth. The false doctrines of Legalism, Mysticism, and Asceticism deceive people into preoccupations with nonsensical, fruitless pursuits after pseudo-spirituality. However, a determination to pursue truth (knowledge of God through His inspired Words) and the will of God for one's life is not an empty pursuit.

"[16] All scripture is given by inspiration of God, and is profitable for doctrine, for reproof, for correction, for instruction in righteousness: [17] That the man of God may be perfect, throughly furnished unto all good works" (II Timothy 3:16-17).

Doctrine establishes God's **normal** expectations for believers. Therefore, doctrine establishes practice. **Reproof** exposes a **deviation** from accepted practice. **Correction** is counter-teaching to **correct a deviation** in doctrine. The epistle to the Colossians is involved in all three, but especially the latter.

Colossians (like the book of Galatians) is intended to correct serious deviations from truth that were trapping and leading people away from accepted norms established by doctrine. God's truth offers no apology for its firmness, and no sympathy for the deceivers. The result of this deception and deviation from the truth is to what

Colossians 2:19-22 refers.

"[19] And not holding the Head, from which all the body by joints and bands having nourishment ministered, and knit together, increaseth with the increase of God. [20] Wherefore if ye be dead with Christ from the rudiments of the world, why, as though living in the world, are ye subject to ordinances, [21] (Touch not; taste not; handle not; [22] Which all are to perish with the using;) after the commandments and doctrines of men" (Colossians 2:19-22)?

Philosophers try to answer all the intellectual questions of the day. Questions like, how is the primitive order of the universe to be restored? Or, what is the origin of evil? In doing so, they forget to ask the most important question. What must I do to be saved? They lose the reality of who Christ is and what He came to do.

DOCTRINE IS THE BASIS OF PRACTICE (COLOSSIANS CHAPTERS 3 AND 4).

Having established the doctrine of completeness in Christ, God begins to establish the practical expectation of that doctrine. Through preaching, or the personal study of the Word, God brings the believer to accept biblical truth (faith). From that point on, He begins to test the believer to see if he has accepted that truth in his life (if faith is real). When practice corresponds with the truth, it becomes a conviction. You cannot say you believe a truth until it changes your thinking, emotions, and actions.

"[23] For if any be a hearer of the word, and not a doer, he is like unto a man beholding his natural face in a glass: [24] For he beholdeth himself, and goeth his way, and straightway forgetteth what manner of man he was. [25] But whoso looketh into the perfect law of liberty, and continueth therein, he being not a forgetful hearer, but a doer of the work, this man shall be blessed in his deed" (James 1:23-25).

THE ADMONITION OF BELIEF OR FAITH (COLOSSIANS 3: 1-2)

The "if ye" question is, if you believe the following, then here is what will take place in your life. The point is this: if you have been spiritually resurrected from among the spiritually dead to a state of spiritual life, then you will be constantly seeking spiritual things. That is quite a statement of expectation, but it is God's expectation. You see, when He says we are to "seek those things which are above," it qualifies itself. "Where Christ sitteth on the right hand of God:" the idea is more than seeking spiritual things above the worldly things, but seeking the exact same things that Christ is seeking. What are those things?

"[1] And Jesus entered and passed through Jericho. [2] And, behold, there was a man named Zacchaeus, which was the chief among the publicans, and he was rich. [3] And he sought to see Jesus who he was; and could not for the press, because he was little of stature. [4] And he ran before, and climbed up into a sycomore tree to see him: for he was to pass that way. [5] And when Jesus came to the place, he looked up, and saw him, and said unto him, Zacchaeus, make haste, and come down; for to day I must abide at thy house. [6] And he made haste, and came down, and received him joyfully. [7] And when they saw it, they all murmured, saying, That he was gone to be guest with a man that is a sinner. [8] And Zacchaeus stood, and said unto the Lord; Behold, Lord, the half of my goods I give to the poor; and if I have taken any thing from any man by false accusation, I restore him fourfold. [9] And Jesus said unto him, This day is salvation come to this house, forsomuch as he also is a son of Abraham. [10] For the Son of man is come to seek and to save that which was lost" (Luke 19:1-10).

Christ is sitting at the "right hand of the Father" - the place of glorification. This signifies His work is "finished." He is seated on the *mercy seat* (the place of propitiation) where we are positionally seated with Christ. For the believer, this is a reminder that the Head is in Heaven (Christ). The body is on earth (the Church, "born again" believers). The work of the "head" is finished (propitiation of God and reconciliation of man). The work of the "body" is the ministry of reconciliation - not to accomplish it, but to preach an accomplished reality.

"Then Jesus said to them again, Peace unto you, as My Father hath sent me, even so send I you" (John 20:21).

BRINGING THE BODY INTO SUBJECTION TO ITS "HEAD" (COLOSSIANS 3:2)

To "set your affection" means to bring one's mind into union with the mind of Christ. This is a rare reality among believers.

> "[19] But I trust in the Lord Jesus to send Timotheus shortly unto you, that I also may be of good comfort, when I know your state. [20] For I have no man likeminded, who will naturally care for your state. [21] For all seek their own, not the things which are Jesus Christ's" (Philippians 2:19-21).

The Christ "life" in us keeps the ministry of Christ through us a priority by bringing glorification and praise to Christ through our actions. Any kind of inconsistency in our lives brings reproach on the name of Christ and upon the ministry. Paul's statement regarding Timothy has been consistently true throughout church history. Trustworthy people with the right priorities are a rare commodity. A person who truly thinks with the mind of Christ puts other people first by an unwillingness to compromise truth.

"NOT ON THE THINGS ON EARTH" (COLOSSIANS 3:2)

The things of this earth are such things as alcohol, tobacco, money, and etc. are not sinful in themselves. The Word does not say that "money is the root of all evil." The Word of God says that - "The love of money is the root of all evil" (I Timothy 6:10). Therefore, the sin problem here is when we become preoccupied with these things. The things of this world are used of Satan to entice us away from serving God. The answer is not to just correct our attitude towards things, but our attitude towards God. Asceticism may take our affection away from the things of the world, but it does not transfer that affection to God.

THE REMINDER (COLOSSIANS 3:3) - "YE ARE DEAD"

The reminder is that, as far as our being "risen with Christ" is concerned, we were separated from all the lusts and enticements of this evil world. We then should be walking in the reality of that resurrected spiritual life. In fact, that reality should be so vivid that the world should not be able to see our old life styles, but only the life of Christ in us and through us. Our old life styles and affections should be "hidden with Christ." As Christ is hidden from the view of the lost world in the Godhead, so should our affections for the things of this world be hidden "with Christ."

CHRIST OUR LIFE (COLOSSIANS 3:4)

Many Christians only *share* their lives with Christ. Christ expects much more than sharing our lives with Him. The meaning of this verse is the heart of practical Christianity. If you were to find some philosophy or formula for an absolutely perfect life in the eyes of God, anyone who believes in that reality would grab for it. It is right here. Stop trying to live your life and let Christ live His life through you. He has given you a new life. He intends for you to give that life away through ministry. That is the only way your life will not be wasted.

If you are not experiencing the fulfillment of a resurrected life "in Christ," let Christ have your life completely. Everything else in this life will prove to be unfulfilling. You can believe the Word of God and protect yourself from wasting more minutes of your precious life by simply determining to live every moment to the glory of God.

Jesus is Lord!

Studies in the Epistle to the Colossians
Chapter Thirteen
SET YOUR AFFECTION ON THINGS ABOVE

1. According to II Timothy 3:16-17, for what three purposes is Bible doctrine given?

2. Which of the above three things is the primary purpose of the book of Colossians?

3. What does accepting any one of the three deceptions listed in chapter twelve (Legalism, Mysticism, or Asceticism) say about a person's understanding of the work of Christ for his salvation?

4. What is God's practical expectation of either teaching or learning spiritual truths (doctrine)?

5. "If ye then be risen with Christ," what is God's expectation of you in that reality?
    A. Why the hypothetical "if"? What is God questioning here?
    B. What should be the evidence of this reality?
    C. "If" you profess to be born again, is this the reality of your life?

6. Read Luke 19:1-10. What does this portion of Scripture reveal to us about the meaning of "seek those things which are above" in Colossians 3:1?

7. What is the theological significance of the fact that Jesus is seated at the "right hand of the Father" in Heaven?

8. What does God expect from believers by the words "set your affection on things above, not on the things of the earth"?

9. What is the meaning of the reminder from Colossians 3:3, "ye are dead"?

10. Can you honestly say Christ is your life? Is doing His will your central purpose for living? If not, what is?

Jesus is Lord!

Studies in the Epistle to the Colossians
Chapter Fourteen
MORTIFICATION OF THE OLD MAN

"[4] When Christ, who is our life, shall appear, then shall ye also appear with him in glory. [5] Mortify therefore your members which are upon the earth; fornication, uncleanness, inordinate affection, evil concupiscence, and covetousness, which is idolatry: [6] For which things' sake the wrath of God cometh on the children of disobedience: [7] In the which ye also walked some time, when ye lived in them. [8] But now ye also put off all these; anger, wrath, malice, blasphemy, filthy communication out of your mouth. [9] Lie not one to another, seeing that ye have put off the old man with his deeds" (Colossians 3:4-9).

THE DAILY TEST OF A RESURRECTED LIFE

Since the believer is "risen with Christ" (Colossians 3:1), God expects the believer to walk and live in the power of a resurrected life. It is from this perspective that we continue in our studies in chapter three. Colossians 3:2-3 establish that the believer is to be completely occupied with Christ. Verse four summarizes that idea with the conclusion that "Christ is in our life." When the believer is completely occupied with the risen Christ, he will live in the power of the Spirit of God and will walk in the power of His holiness.

Before we can continue and understand the balance of the epistle there is one singular principle that is necessary for our comprehension of the text. **We do not live the life of Christ. He lives our life.** When this takes place, there is always a tendency for a self-righteous attitude. It is necessary to maintain a proper perspective of whom and what we are in our "flesh." We need to get a view of God like Isaiah did and then compare ourselves to God rather than other people.

"[1] In the year that king Uzziah died I saw also the Lord

120

sitting upon a throne, high and lifted up, and his train filled the temple. [2] Above it stood the seraphims: each one had six wings; with twain he covered his face, and with twain he covered his feet, and with twain he did fly. [3] And one cried unto another, and said, Holy, holy, holy, is the LORD of hosts: the whole earth is full of his glory. [4] And the posts of the door moved at the voice of him that cried, and the house was filled with smoke. [5] Then said I, Woe is me! for I am undone; because I am a man of unclean lips, and I dwell in the midst of a people of unclean lips: for mine eyes have seen the King, the LORD of hosts" (Isaiah 6:1-5).

Isaiah's vision of God in His glory resulted in two appropriate evaluations - one of himself and the other of those to whom he ministered.

1. "I am a man of unclean lips."
2. "I dwell among a people of unclean lips."

THE PRACTICE OF "CHRIST OUR LIFE"

When Christ is our life as a spiritual reality (practice), it will be our desire to "mortify" the sin nature (Colossians 3:5).

"[2] For the law of the Spirit of life in Christ Jesus hath made me free from the law of sin and death. [3] For what the law could not do, in that it was weak through the flesh, God sending his own Son in the likeness of sinful flesh, and for sin, condemned sin in the flesh: [4] That the righteousness of the law might be fulfilled in us, who walk not after the flesh, but after the Spirit" (Romans 8:2-4).

We should never confuse our practical responsibility with our concrete position in Christ. Our position never changes and is unaffected by our response to God's expectation. It is our love for God and thankfulness for that eternal position ("complete in Christ") that should motivate us to obedience.

The word "mortify" is not talking about suicide. The emphasis is putting the *carnal mind* (the sin nature) to death. Since our mind and thoughts control our bodies, the mind of which Christ is in control will control the body He possesses.

"³ For though we walk in the flesh, we do not war after the flesh: ⁴ (For the weapons of our warfare are not carnal, but mighty through God to the pulling down of strong holds;) ⁵ Casting down imaginations, and every high thing that exalteth itself against the knowledge of God, and bringing into captivity every thought to the obedience of Christ; ⁶ And having in a readiness to revenge all disobedience, when your obedience is fulfilled" (II Corinthians 10:3-6).

In Colossians 3:5, the word "members" refers to the parts of the body as they are employed in life actions (in this case, sin). These "members" employ themselves in four described sinful practices.

1. "Fornication" is sexual immorality outside of the confines of a husband\wife relationship.
2. "Uncleanness" is any moral impurity resulting from the gratification of selfish desires.
3. "Inordinate affection" is described in Romans 1:26-32 - especially referring to sexual perversions.

"²⁶ For this cause God gave them up unto vile affections: for even their women did change the natural use into that which is against nature: ²⁷ And likewise also the men, leaving the natural use of the woman, burned in their lust one toward another; men with men working that which is unseemly, and receiving in themselves that recompence of their error which was meet. ²⁸ And even as they did not like to retain God in *their* knowledge, God gave them over to a reprobate mind, to do those things which are not convenient; ²⁹ Being filled with all unrighteousness, fornication, wickedness, covetousness, maliciousness; full of envy, murder, debate, deceit, malignity; whisperers, ³⁰Backbiters, haters of God, despiteful, proud, boasters, inventors of evil things, disobedient to parents, ³¹ Without understanding, covenantbreakers, without natural affection, implacable, unmerciful: ³² Who knowing the judgment of God, that they which commit such things are worthy of death, not only do the same, but have pleasure in them that do them" (Romans 1:26-32).

4. "Covetousness" carries climactic force in the Greek and could actually read "especially covetousness." It is a category of sin that stands by itself called *idolatry*.

Covetousness is the greedy desire to have more than a person needs. It is the epitome of ungratefulness. It is the religion of the discontent - the *complainer*.

Our incentive to "mortify" the desires of our flesh should be the return of Christ (Colossians 3:4). The Lordship of Jesus is not a visible sovereignty. Unless our lives' actions (culturally and distinctively in the areas of personal holiness) make His Lordship visible, His Lordship will remain invisible. Jesus is personally hidden from the lost world because believers refuse to live the "life of Christ." When we sin, we are hiding Christ from the world He died to redeem. It is a wonderful truth to know the *all-sufficiency* of Jesus, but it is a sad fact that we all too often do not manifest the *all-supremacy* of Jesus.

THE PROBLEM BETWEEN POSITION (COMPLETE IN CHRIST) AND THE PRACTICAL (CHRIST OUR LIFE)

Positionally the believer is "risen with Christ" (v. 1), but practically we live in a tension between what Christ has already completed and what is not yet complete (our glorification, v. 4). We are regenerated to be a colony of holiness in Christ and God expects us to manifest His holiness to a culture of evil corruption. We are to be as bright as a lighted city set on a hill.

When our lives are no different from the rest of the lost world, we lose our distinctiveness as the residing place of the Shekinah Glory of God in the indwelling Holy Spirit. As a result, those dying in the darkness of spiritual blindness cannot see the light. If you will dedicate your lives to Christ Jesus, your city may not like you, it may not break down the doors of your church to get in, but they will know your church exists "to seek and save the lost." Those in the darkness will be able to clearly see the "city set on the hill" distinctively different, distinctively separated, and distinctively holy.

ACCORDING TO COLOSSIANS 3:5, ANY SIN IN OUR LIVES DENIES THE LORDSHIP OF JESUS OVER LIVES.

When we allow the sin nature to rule in our lives, we actually displace Jesus from His place of rule with our willful selfishness. Any form of immorality is an opposite of biblical love. Any form of immorality is nothing more than manipulative, willful, and exploitive selfishness.

ACCORDING TO COLOSSIANS 3:6, CHASTENING IS INTENDED TO CORRECT IN ORDER TO RESTORE THE BRIGHTNESS OF TRUTH AND MAINTAIN THE BELIEVER'S SPIRITUAL DISTINCTIVENESS.

"[1] Be ye therefore followers of God, as dear children; [2] And walk in love, as Christ also hath loved us, and hath given himself for us an offering and a sacrifice to God for a sweetsmelling savour. [3] But fornication, and all uncleanness, or covetousness, let it not be once named among you, as becometh saints; [4] Neither filthiness, nor foolish talking, nor jesting, which are not convenient: but rather giving of thanks. [5] For this ye know, that no whoremonger, nor unclean person, nor covetous man, who is an idolater, hath any inheritance in the kingdom of Christ and of God. [6] Let no man deceive you with vain words: for because of these things cometh the wrath of God upon the children of disobedience. [7] Be not ye therefore partakers with them. [8] For ye were sometimes darkness, but now are ye light in the Lord: walk as children of light" (Ephesians 5:1-8).

If you are deceived into the ways of life listed in Ephesians 5:3-5, you become a son of disobedience and you can expect God's chastening.

"For whom the Lord loveth He chasteneth, and scourgeth every son whom He recieveth" (Hebrews 12: 6).

The "wrath of God" never comes on a child of God. The kinds of practices listed in Ephesians 5:3-5 reveal the life of an unbeliever ("children of disobedience," Ephesians 5:6). The word "them" of Colossians 5:7 specifically refers to unbelievers. Colossians 5:8 expands upon "them" referring to them as being part of the "darkness." Therefore, it is completely abnormal for a child of God to be involved in anything listed in Ephesians 5:3-5. Such practices even manifest self-deception regarding salvation and being "born again."

Jesus is Lord!

Studies in the Epistle to the Colossians
Chapter Fourteen
MORTIFICATION OF THE OLD MAN

1. What statement of Colossians 3:1 gives us the perspective of the expectation of God for the rest of the epistle?

2. What statement of Colossians 3:4 summarizes verses 1-4?

3. What singular principle is necessary to understand before we can understand the expectations of God in the balance of the epistle?

4. What is the *Isaiah Complex* (Isaiah 6:5) and why is it necessary that the believer maintain it when Christ is living His life through him?

5. According to Colossians 3:5, what will be the result when "Christ is our life"?

6. Why should we be careful to distinguish between our practical responsibility and our concrete position ("complete") in Christ?

7. Read II Corinthians 10:5. How does this verse clarify God's expectations of the word "mortify" in Colossians 3:5?

8. What are some ways a person's "members" are employed in sin according to Colossians 3:8-9?

9. When Christ is not our life, why is He hidden from the world? What is the believer supposed to be (*when Christ is his life*) that reveals Jesus to the lost world?

10. When a believer allows his sin nature to rule in his life, what happens to the Lordship of Jesus?

11. Read Hebrews 12:6. What happens when a believer sins?

12. What does the word "them" mean in the context of those practicing the things listed in Ephesians 5:3-5 as one of the "children of disobedience"?

Jesus is Lord!

Studies in the Epistle to the Colossians
Chapter Fifteen
THE CHRISTIAN'S PRIORITY

"[10] And have put on the new *man*, which is renewed in knowledge after the image of him that created him: [11] Where there is neither Greek nor Jew, circumcision nor uncircumcision, Barbarian, Scythian, bond *nor* free: but Christ *is* all, and in all" (Colossians 3:10-11).

These verses might be amplified as follows: "[10] And having enveloped yourself with the new life in Christ, the resurrected life, the one that is re-created with a full and maturing knowledge in the likeness of the image of Jesus, Who the knowledge reflects, and Who is the One by whom you were recreated. [11] In which state, namely the resurrected life, there cannot be any prejudicial or cultural indifferences such as this cultural differences of the Jew and the Greek, the religious differences between the circumcised and the uncircumcised, the intellectual or educational differences that divide the Barbarian from the Scythian or the social differences that divide the slave man from the free man, but Christ is our common denominator, He has obliterated all cultural and religious distinctions, all intellectual elitism, all social classes, and has substituted Himself for all of these, and He alone should occupy the full spectrum of our human existence and fully saturate all that our existence becomes."

THE REALIZATION OF THE LORDSHIP OF CHRIST IN OUR LIFE (COLOSSIANS 3:10-11)

If we have been saved ("born again"), we recognize the authority that Jesus has over our lives. We should recognize His right of Lordship. If that has taken place, we have agreed to *envelope* our lives in the Word of God (v. 10, "put on"). The instant we are saved, we become a "new creation" (II Corinthians 5:17). However, this is only the beginning of a lifelong process of renewal (Romans 12:2, *metamorphosis*). This process is one of education and practical sanctification (*spiritual growth and faith building*). The Bible calls this "edification." It is building the believer up in the areas of spiritual maturity and godliness. By this, the believer is progressively transfigured into *Christlikeness*.

"[12] Not as though I had already attained, either were already perfect: but I follow after, if that I may apprehend that for which also I am apprehended of Christ Jesus. [13] Brethren, I count not myself to have apprehended: but this one thing I do, forgetting those things which are behind, and reaching forth unto those things which are before, [14] I press toward the mark for the prize of the high calling of God in Christ Jesus. [15] Let us therefore, as many as be perfect, be thus minded: and if in any thing ye be otherwise minded, God shall reveal even this unto you.[16] Nevertheless, whereto we have already attained, let us walk by the same rule, let us mind the same thing" (Philippians. 3:12-16).

This process of spiritual growth (edification or progressive transfiguration) involves two requirements of the believer before maturity can be realized (Philippians 3:13).

1. "Forgetting those things which are behind" - putting behind us all beliefs or practices that would hinder us from full maturity or to remove from our life anything that might keep us from growing to spiritual maturity.
2. "Reaching forth unto those things which are before" - stretching ourselves to achieve goals.

A *watchman* must keep my eyes fixed upon Jesus, his "mark." Christlikeness is a standard of spiritual maturity. The Christian must "press" (or push) himself to that goal. The goal (Christlikeness) is his "prize" (Philippians 3:14).

If you want Christian maturity, it will have to be something you want more than anything else. Anything that would hinder spiritual maturity must be put away. Anything that would expedite spiritual maturity must become a priority. It is to this latter point that Colossians 3:12 refers.

THE EMPHATIC COMMAND FOR MATURITY (COLOSSIANS 3:12)

"Put on" refers to the resurrected life of Christ available to the believer in active co-operation with the indwelling Holy Spirit. When Christ was resurrected from the dead, He provided much more to the believer than victory over death (*as great as that is*). He provides the availability of the resurrected life of Christ to the believer in the Person of the indwelling Holy Spirit.

"[7] If ye abide in me, and my words abide in you, ye shall ask what ye will, and it shall be done unto you. [8] Herein is my Father glorified, that ye bear much fruit; so shall ye be my disciples. [9] As the Father hath loved me, so have I loved you: continue ye in my love. [10] If ye keep my commandments, ye shall abide in my love; even as I have kept my Father's commandments, and abide in his love. [11] These things have I spoken unto you, that my joy might remain in you, and that your joy might be full. [12] This is my commandment, That ye love one another, as I have loved you. [13] Greater love hath no man than this, that a man lay down his life for his friends" (John 15:7-13).

1. John 15:7 - **The promise**
2. John 15: 9-10 - **The proposal**
3 John 15: 11 - **The purpose**
4. John 15: 12-13 - **The proclamation**

THE RESURRECTED LIFE OF JESUS (JOHN 14:15-21)

"[15] If ye love me, keep my commandments. [16] And I will pray the Father, and he shall give you another Comforter, that he may abide with you for ever; [17] Even the Spirit of truth; whom the world cannot receive, because it seeth him not, neither knoweth him: but ye know him; for he dwelleth with you, and shall be in you. [18] I will not leave you comfortless: I will come to you. [19] Yet a little while, and the world seeth me no more; but ye see me: because I live, ye shall live also. [20] At that day ye shall know that I

am in my Father, and ye in me, and I in you. [21] He that
hath my commandments, and keepeth them, he it is that
loveth me: and he that loveth me shall be loved of my
Father, and I will love him, and will manifest myself to
him" (John 14:15-21).

1. Verse 19 - "Because I {*Jesus*} live, ye shall live also."
2. Verse 20 - "At that day {*when you begin to live the
resurrected life*} ye shall know."

According to Colossians 3:12, to "put on" the
resurrected life is to become so possessed of the mind of
Christ that in thought, feeling, and action you begin to
resemble Him. In doing so, you begin to reproduce His life
in you.

"Put on" is in the aorist tense and imperative mood
in the Greek. That means it is a command that should be
obeyed at once. It should be given first priority. It should
supersede all other needs or relationships. There should be
nothing more important in your life than allowing Christ to
live His life through us.

The word "elect" refers to our position "in Christ" -
our place of service in ministry (the priesthood of the
believer). Therefore, the main priority of the "elect" is
doing "the work of the ministry," which involves
proclaiming the message of salvation and making disciples
of those saved. This is accomplished by the preaching of
the Gospel of Jesus Christ.

THE CHARACTERISTICS OF GOD'S CHOSEN PRIESTS (COLOSSIANS 3:12)

"Holy" means separated from the world and unto
God. The believer is specifically and distinctively chosen
to serve God. Holy is a term referring to God's children.
What the believer is *positionally* is what he *should be
practically*.

"[11] O ye Corinthians, our mouth is open unto you, our heart
is enlarged. [12] Ye are not straitened in us, but ye are
straitened in your own bowels. [13] Now for a recompence in
the same, (I speak as unto my children,) be ye also
enlarged. [14] Be ye not unequally yoked together with

unbelievers: for what fellowship hath righteousness with unrighteousness? and what communion hath light with darkness? [15] And what concord hath Christ with Belial? or what part hath he that believeth with an infidel? [16] And what agreement hath the temple of God with idols? for ye are the temple of the living God; as God hath said, I will dwell in them, and walk in them; and I will be their God, and they shall be my people. [17] Wherefore come out from among them, and be ye separate, saith the Lord, and touch not the unclean thing; and I will receive you, [18] And will be a Father unto you, and ye shall be my sons and daughters, saith the Lord Almighty" (II Corinthians 6:11-18).

"Having therefore these promises, dearly beloved, let us cleanse ourselves from all filthiness of the flesh and spirit, perfecting holiness in the fear of God" (II Corinthians 7:1).

The word "beloved" in II Corinthians 7:1 refers to those who are the divinely loved children of God.

"[1] My little children, these things write I unto you, that ye sin not. And if any man sin, we have an advocate with the Father, Jesus Christ the righteous: [2] And he is the propitiation for our sins: and not for ours only, but also for the sins of the whole world. [3] And hereby we do know that we know him, if we keep his commandments. [4] He that saith, I know him, and keepeth not his commandments, is a liar, and the truth is not in him. [5] But whoso keepeth his word, in him verily is the love of God perfected: hereby know we that we are in him. [6] He that saith he abideth in him ought himself also so to walk, even as he walked" (I John 2:1-6).

PUTTING ON THE RESURRECTED LIFE IS PUTTING ON CHRIST
(Seven Qualities of Spiritual Maturity - Colossians 3:12)

1. The words "bowels of mercies" refer to the heart of Christ (*compassion*).

"For we have not an high priest which cannot be touched with the feeling of our infirmities; but was in all points tempted like as we are, yet without sin" (Hebrews 4:15).

2. The word "kindness" refers to a gentle, full of grace disposition.

"Father forgive them; for they know not what they do" (Luke 23:34).

3. The words "humbleness of mind" refer to a submissive spirit.

"Let nothing be done through strife or vainglory; but in lowliness of mind let each esteem other better than themselves" (Philippians 2:3).

4. Meekness is not weakness. Meekness is having the power to do what you want to do, while submitting yourself to what is best for others first. There is a desire engrained in every one of us to be on the *top of the heap*. That kind of attitude is the opposite of meekness.

"[27] And whosoever will be chief among you, let him be your servant: [28] Even as the Son of man came not to be ministered unto, but to minister, and to give his life a ransom for many" (Matthew 20:27-28).

5. "Longsuffering" with others is the willingness to patiently endure, even under ill-treatment.

"[15] This is a faithful saying, and worthy of all acceptation, that Christ Jesus came into the world to save sinners; of whom I am chief. [16] Howbeit for this cause I obtained mercy, that in me first Jesus Christ might shew forth all longsuffering, for a pattern to them which should hereafter believe on him to life everlasting" (I Timothy. 1: 15-16).

6. "Forbearing"

7. "Forgiving

In Colossians 3:13a, "forbearing" and "forgiving" mean to endure wrong for right's sake (*full of grace*). To what degree are we to forbear and forgive (Colossians 3:13b)? We are to forbear and forgive to the same degree that Christ forbears and forgives us - completely.

In Colossians 3:14, we see that all other virtues other than love are only *undergarments*. They are functional, but love is the *outer garment*. Love is the garment of *esthetic value*. Love is what gives Christianity its *appeal*. Love is what makes others want what we have (the resurrected Christ life). Love is the *bonding agent* for all other virtues. It is the garment that holds all other garments in there right places.

"Perfectness" refers to our practical maturity. True Christian love is the central outward manifestation of that spiritual maturity. We are *positionally* complete in every way in Christ. When we "put on" Christ, we are *practically* complete in every aspect. When that happens, our life manifests that completeness to the world. This is what God wants from every believer. This is His priority for our life. Therefore, this *should* be the priority of our lives.

Jesus is Lord!

Studies in the Epistle to the Colossians
Chapter Fifteen
THE CHRISTIAN'S PRIORITY

1. The instant we are saved we become "new creation." Does that mean every bad habit and all our wrong thinking will also be immediately removed?

2. What is the Bible word for education and spiritual growth that is intent on spiritual maturity?

3. According to Philippians 3:13, what two "things" are necessary before spiritual maturity can be realized?

4. According to Philippians 3:14, what is the "mark" we are to "press toward"?
    A. What does the word "press" mean in this context?
    B. What is the goal of all of this?
    C. What is the "prize" for accomplishing this?

5. Read Colossians 3:12. What specifically is the believer to "put on" that is available to all yielded believers?

6. What is the **promise** of John 15:7?

7. What is the **proposal** of John 15:9-10?

8. What is the **purpose** revealed in John 15:11?

9. What is the **proclamation** of John 15:12-13?

10. Read John 14:20. At what "day" will the believer "know" this?

11. Define the following two characteristics of God's chosen servants.
    A. "Holy"
    B. "Beloved"

12. List seven things from Colossians 3:12-14 that will be characteristic of a believer that has "put on" the resurrected Christ life.op

Jesus is Lord!

Studies in the Epistle to the Colossians
Chapter Sixteen
WHEN GOD'S WORD IS AT HOME
IN OUR HEARTS

"[14] And above all these things *put on* charity, which is the bond of perfectness. [15] And let the peace of God rule in your hearts, to the which also ye are called in one body; and be ye thankful. [16] Let the word of Christ dwell in you richly in all wisdom; teaching and admonishing one another in psalms and hymns and spiritual songs, singing with grace in your hearts to the Lord. [17] And whatsoever ye do in word or deed, *do* all in the name of the Lord Jesus, giving thanks to God and the Father by him" (Colossians 3:14-17).

In the first two chapters of the epistle to the Colossians, God has shown us the distinctives of a Bible believing Christian. He has shown us the particular beliefs that distinguish Bible-believing Christians from all other religious beliefs. **Some of these are:**

1. Separation from false religious beliefs; the emphasis here is not to allow the influences of false religions. If we allow this, these influences will absorb us and cause us to lose our distinctiveness (Colossians 1:24-29).
2. Beliefs that hold to the distinct uniqueness of Jesus Christ (Colossians 1:15-23) will keep us from corruption.
3. There is a biblical expectation of a new life for true believers (Colossians 2:1-8).
4. There is the biblical distinction of total, absolute "completeness in Christ" for the true believer (Colossians 2:9-13) over all false beliefs
5. There are three contradictions to the believer's completeness in Christ:

    A. Legalism, Colossians 3:14-17
    B. Mysticism, Colossians 2:18-19
    C. Asceticism, Colossians 2:20-23

In chapters three through four, the instruction moves from doctrinal distinctiveness to the expected and corresponding change in life style, or a **PRACTICAL DISTINCTIVENESS.**

Going back to verse twelve of chapter three, the command "put on" calls for a firm determination to practice, or manifest in our life styles, what we are positionally in Christ (2:10).

THE GIRDLE OF LOVE (COLOSSIANS 3:14)

In the Middle East, people wore very loose garments because of the heat and humidity. In order to travel (*which was usually done by walking*) they would *gird up their loins*. A person who allowed his garments to be loose and who would not gird up his loins would make very little progress on his journey. We should have an open mind to the things of God's Word, and a closed mind to the philosophies of the world.

> "[13] Wherefore gird up the loins of your mind, be sober, and hope to the end for the grace that is to be brought unto you at the revelation of Jesus Christ; [14] As obedient children, not fashioning yourselves according to the former lusts in your ignorance: [15] But as he which hath called you is holy, so be ye holy in all manner of conversation; [16] Because it is written, Be ye holy; for I am holy" (I Peter 1:13-16).

Therefore, this metaphor of girding ourselves with "charity" speaks of the love of Christ which constrains us to be obedient.

> "[14] For the love of Christ constraineth us; because we thus judge, that if one died for all, then were all dead: [15] And that he died for all, that they which live should not henceforth live unto themselves, but unto him which died for them, and rose again" (II Corinthians 5:14-15).

This refers to the virtues of Colossians 3:5-13 and to the environment in which we live. Virtues are useless unless they are applied to relationships. Love holds all of these virtues in a proper perspective. This kind of love is distinctively Christian. This kind of love finds its only source in God. It is implanted within the child of God in the Person of the indwelling Holy Spirit.

"[14] We know that we have passed from death unto life, because we love the brethren. He that loveth not his brother abideth in death. [15] Whosoever hateth his brother is a murderer: and ye know that no murderer hath eternal life abiding in him. [16] Hereby perceive we the love of God, because he laid down his life for us: and we ought to lay down our lives for the brethren. [17] But whoso hath this world's good, and seeth his brother have need, and shutteth up his bowels of compassion from him, how dwelleth the love of God in him? [18] My little children, let us not love in word, neither in tongue; but in deed and in truth. [19] And hereby we know that we are of the truth, and shall assure our hearts before him" (I John 3:14-19).

"[7] Beloved, let us love one another: for love is of God; and every one that loveth is born of God, and knoweth God. [8] He that loveth not knoweth not God; for God is love. [9] In this was manifested the love of God toward us, because that God sent his only begotten Son into the world, that we might live through him. [10] Herein is love, not that we loved God, but that he loved us, and sent his Son to be the propitiation for our sins" (I John 4:7-10).

Biblical love is not the mindless, universal acceptance of all beliefs systems within the *Christian* community. Some of these beliefs directly contradict the Word of God. In fact, many of the epistles, like the epistle to the Colossians, were written to correct false beliefs we are now asked to blindly accept as simply other acceptable alternatives.

"[5] And now I beseech thee, lady, not as though I wrote a new commandment unto thee, but that which we had from the beginning, that we love one another. [6] And this is love, that we walk after his commandments. This is the commandment, That, as ye have heard from the beginning, ye should walk in it. [7] For many deceivers are entered into the world, who confess not that Jesus Christ is come in the flesh. This is a deceiver and an antichrist. [8] Look to yourselves, that we lose not those things which we have wrought, but that we receive a full reward. [9] Whosoever transgresseth, and abideth not in the doctrine of Christ, hath not God. He that abideth in the doctrine of Christ, he hath both the Father and the Son. [10] If there come any unto you, and bring not this doctrine, receive him not into your house, neither bid him God speed: [11] For he that biddeth him God speed is partaker of his evil deeds" (II John 1:5-11).

"I have no greater joy than to hear that my children walk in truth" (III John 1:4).

Love is the bond of "perfectness" (maturity, or practical completeness). It has been said that *no believer has achieved spiritual maturity until all of his works are thoroughly encompassed with love.* "Bond" is from the Greek word *sundesmos* (soon'-des-mos). It means that which binds together, a band, bond of ligaments by which the members of the human body are united together; or that which is bound together, a bundle. In the context, it refers to Christian love as the bonding agent of spiritually mature believers. Love is defined as sacrificial obedience to the Lordship of Christ through the leading of the indwelling Holy Spirit and the Word of God.

GOD'S PEACE IS A PRACTICAL MANIFESTATION OF PRACTICAL COMPLETENESS OR SPIRITUAL MATURITY (COLOSSIANS 3:15-17).

God's peace will rule our emotions (v. 15). When the circumstances of life seem overwhelming, we become anxious. Anxiety is the opposite of trust. When that happens, God's peace is not ruling our hearts. Christ should be more than the Lord of our salvation. We must allow Him to be Lord of our emotions. When that happens, God's peace will protect us from the influences of the harmful circumstances of life. When God's peace does not rule our hearts, the difficulties intended to increase our faith tend to have the opposite effect. Those difficulties become erasers of faith.

God's peace will rule our hearts. When that happens we have accepted Romans 8:28.

"And we know that all things work together for good to

them that love God, to them who are the called according to his purpose."

It is God's peace that **unites** believers (Colossians 3:15b). Having God's peace refers to an inter-dependency of believers responsible to and for one another.

"[11] Wherefore comfort yourselves together, and edify one another, even as also ye do. [12] And we beseech you, brethren, to know them which labour among you, and are over you in the Lord, and admonish you; [13] And to esteem them very highly in love for their work's sake. And be at peace among yourselves. [14] Now we exhort you, brethren, warn them that are unruly, comfort the feebleminded, support the weak, be patient toward all men. [15] See that none render evil for evil unto any man; but ever follow that which is good, both among yourselves, and to all men" (I Thessalonians 5:11-15).

God's peace is a peace that generates **thankfulness** in the lives of believers (Colossians 3:15c). The person who understands that God's working in his life is for his good, will become a thankful person.

"In every thing give thanks: for this is the will of God in Christ Jesus concerning you" (I Thessalonians 5:18).

THE REIGNING WORD OF GOD (COLOSSIANS 3:16A) - "Let the word of Christ dwell in you"

The "word of Christ" is synonymous with the Word of the Lord.

"For from you sounded out the word of the Lord not only in Macedonia and Achaia, but also in every place your faith to God–ward is spread abroad; so that we need not to speak any thing" (I Thessalonians 1:8).

What is God's expectation of believers according to the command, "let the word of Christ dwell in you? The Word of Christ is the life-directing command of the Lord to be unquestionably obeyed.

The word "dwell" literally means *to be at home.* It does not refer to a mere visit. It refers to allowing the Lord Jesus to sovereignly govern our lives through His Word. A subject of a sovereign understands that all he owned or claimed was at the directive of the sovereign who held all real rights to that property. That is the idea here.

The word "richly" means that it should not be a burden to submit to the Word of Christ. The Word of Christ should be considered a *high prize* and greatly appreciated. A believer must realize that there cannot be any real value in life if the Word of Christ is not highly prized and obeyed. Without it, we are nothing more than spiritual paupers regardless of any material wealth we may possess. The greatest of all riches is to know Christ. The greatest act of benevolence is to preach Christ so others might know Him.

TWO PRACTICAL APPLICATIONS FOR ALLOWING THE WORD OF CHRIST TO REIGN (COLOSSIANS 3:16B)

1. In the words, "in wisdom teaching," wisdom is centered in Christ (*applicationally*), while teaching emphasizes instruction in the practical application of the Word of Christ.
2. "Admonishing one another" refers to the willingness of fellow believers to receive warning and correction from one another.

When Christ's Word is at home in our lives, these two things will be a welcomed practical reality.

METHODS OF TEACHING AND ADMONISHMENT

1. Psalms and hymns in music

We can teach with poetry and song. These two vehicles of teaching have historically embraced all forms of biblical truth with the intent of promoting spiritual and emotional response from the child of God pertinent to the character and nature of God.

The "singing" of Psalms is intended to be a means by which the child of God expresses verbally that which is a reality in his heart. The "singing" of Psalms was the musical expression of doctrinal beliefs about who God is and our faith in Him. "Singing" is a means to express the testimonies of a believer's faith and beliefs. "Singing" was to be done (v. 16) "to the Lord," and not to entertain or impress men. This is a central principle governing the use of music in worship. If the purpose of "singing" is intended to make you *feel good,* it is not biblical music (v. 17).

Whatsoever you say "in word" or do "in deed" should only be done when you have the complete approval of Christ by the authority of His inspired Word (Colossians 3:17).

Jesus is Lord!

Studies in the Epistle to the Colossians
Chapter Sixteen
WHEN GOD'S WORD IS AT HOME
IN OUR HEARTS

1. What is the difference between **doctrinal distinctiveness** and **practical distinctiveness**?

2. What is the relationship of the practical command to "put on" in Colossians 3:12 to the doctrinal truth of Colossians 2:10?

3. What is the meaning behind the metaphor of *the girdle of love* used in Colossians 3:14?

4. Read II Corinthians 5:14-15. Many times love is used as an excuse to allow Christians to do things that really are unscriptural. In what way is true Christian love intended to constrain the believer?

5. From the context of your answer to the above question, how do the virtues of Colossians 3:5-13 relate to biblical love? According to I John 3:14-19 and 4:7-10, what is the only source of true Christian love and how does a person possess it?

6. Read II John 1:5-11 and III John 1:4. What do these verses have to say about the false notion that love is the universal acceptance of all beliefs within the *Christian* community?

7. List three ways from Colossians 3:15 in which the product of God's peace is a practical manifestation of spiritual maturity in the life of a believer.

8. Describe in what way the Word of Christ dwells in the life of a believer. Discuss what that means practically.

9. From Colossians 3:16b, what are the two practical applications of allowing the Word of Christ to reign in your life?

Jesus is Lord!

Studies in the Epistle to the Colossians
Chapter Seventeen
ALL IN THE NAME OF THE LORD JESUS

"[16] Let the word of Christ dwell in you richly in all wisdom; teaching and admonishing one another in psalms and hymns and spiritual songs, singing with grace in your hearts to the Lord. [17] And whatsoever ye do in word or deed, *do* all in the name of the Lord Jesus, giving thanks to God and the Father by him" (Colossians 3:16-17).

In Colossians 3:16, we are instructed to allow the Word of Christ to be at home in our lives, to be an intricate and governing, ruling, and reigning force in our lives.

The Word of God is to be considered and treated as a *member of the family*. It should have a permanent place in our lives. It should be more than a book to us. The idea implied is one of an intimate relationship. We should be working to know the Word of God as intimately as we seek to know our husband, wife, or child.

When that happens, the Word of God becomes more than a fixture in our lives. It becomes an intricate part of who and what we are as a person. It will become such an intimately interwoven part of what we are that no one will be able to distinguish where we end and it begins.

The word "richly" signifies an overflowing abundance like an overflowing treasure chest. The words "wisdom teaching" signify that the overflowing of the wealth of the Word of God is to flow out of our lives with direction and purpose. The direction and purpose of the overflowing wealth of the truth of God's Word from our lives is intended to be directed to specific individuals. In other words, we are not to be treasure chests for truth, but distribution centers.

"[17] Charge them that are rich in this world, that they be not highminded, nor trust in uncertain riches, but in the living

God, who giveth us richly all things to enjoy; [18] That they do good, that they be rich in good works, ready to distribute, willing to communicate" (I Timothy 6:17-18).

What God teaches us, we are to teach to others. Wisdom is the application of knowledge. It is the heart and mind of God overflowing from the life of a believer yielded to the Holy Spirit. To have wisdom does not necessarily make you wise. It is the application and use of wisdom in everyday life that makes a person wise. Solomon had wisdom. When he used it, he was wise. When he didn't use it, he was not wise. The book of Ecclesiastes is the history of unused wisdom and the consequences of that on a life.

"[17] And I gave my heart to know wisdom, and to know madness and folly: I perceived that this also is vexation of spirit. [18] For in much wisdom is much grief: and he that increaseth knowledge increaseth sorrow" (Ecclesiastes 1:17-18).

The emphasis of teaching wisdom is not merely factual, but applicational. Doctrine teaches us more than facts. It applies the facts to life, forming applications and establishing principles and gives answers and solutions to the everyday situations of life.

The words "admonishing one another" emphasize a warning of exhortation with the intention to encourage, reprove or correct, or even to find fault (I Corinthians 5:12-6:5).

"[12] For what have I to do to judge them also that are without? do not ye judge them that are within? [13] But them that are without God judgeth. Therefore put away from among yourselves that wicked person. [1] Dare any of you, having a matter against another, go to law before the unjust, and not before the saints? [2] Do ye not know that the saints shall judge the world? and if the world shall be judged by you, are ye unworthy to judge the smallest matters? [3] Know ye not that we shall judge angels? how much more things that pertain to this life? [4] If then ye have judgments of things pertaining to this life, set them to judge who are least esteemed in the church. [5] I speak to your shame. Is it so, that there is not a wise man among you? no, not one that shall be able to judge between his brethren" (I Corinthians 5:12-6:5)?

METHODS OF TEACHING AND ADMONISHING

"Psalms and hymns and spiritual songs" - each of these refers to the inspired Psalms of the Old Testament. The Psalms of the Old Testament are a source of great practical truths. Psalms are intended to be doctrine with musical accompaniment. Hymns are songs of praise to God and refer to the Psalms that were sung. Another name for the Psalms was the Book of Hymns. Spiritual songs are songs with or without music on any spiritual subject.

When the Word of Christ dwells in us "richly," it will naturally burst forth in our life like music, as the Psalms did in David's life. What fills our minds will fill our hearts. What fills our hearts will fill our lives.

"[19] Lay not up for yourselves treasures upon earth, where moth and rust doth corrupt, and where thieves break through and steal: [20] But lay up for yourselves treasures in heaven, where neither moth nor rust doth corrupt, and where thieves do not break through nor steal: [21] For where your treasure is, there will your heart be also" (Matthew 6:19-21).

The words "with grace in your hearts" signify that grace is a divine attribute owned and distributed only by God. When grace is in the believer's life, it is divinely supplied. It is the divine energy produced in the heart of the believer yielded to the Holy Spirit.

Singing that is done for the purpose of entertainment or self-glorification is of the flesh and is not done out of the grace in our heart. The idea here is to make sure the focus of music is upon worshipping God. The central purpose of singing is to glorify God, not to display one's voice or musical abilities. The focal point is the message about the Lord, not upon the sound.

"In your hearts" means to *sing from the heart*. True praise cannot be manufactured. True praise is the overflow of our gratefulness to God. True praise cannot be withheld.

It must be expressed.

"TO THE LORD"

Praising God is not for people or to people, although other people may be present. Praise directs itself to Jesus our Lord. Praising God is so focused on God it becomes almost oblivious to other people around us.

All too often, the music that is sung and played in God's assembly house is the world's music written to please and entertain the world, not to glorify God. The words are familiarly Christian, but the music is the world's. Much of today's Christian music is not written to glorify God for worship or praise. Much of today's Christian music is written for entertainment, not for a close encounter with God. The command to be "in the world, but not of it" applies also to our music.

"WHATEVER YE DO IN WORD OR DEED, DO ALL IN THE NAME OF THE LORD JESUS" (COLOSSIANS 3:17).

This statement follows in context from the previous statements above. The Lordship of Jesus must be the springboard for everything we do. We have His authority when anything is done in His name. The "name" of the Lord Jesus stands for all that He is and all that He has done. The "name" of the Lord Jesus speaks of His sufficiency to meet our every need. As Christians, everything we do in this life is done in His name and reflects on His name.

A great deal of what is being done in His name today degrades His name. It does not exalt it. What does it mean in our society to be called a Christian? The individual who is doing "all in the name of Jesus" is acting in total conformity to the Word of His proclaimed Lord, and doing so with "thanksgiving."

Jesus is Lord!

Studies in the Epistle to the Colossians
Chapter Seventeen
ALL IN THE NAME OF THE LORD JESUS

1. In Colossians 3:16, what does God mean by "Let the Word of Christ dwell in you"?
    A. Do you think this command is a reality in your life?
    B. If yes, what makes you think so?

2. What does the word "richly" signify about the abundance of the Word of God in our lives?

3. The words "in all wisdom; teaching" reveal that the overflow of the wealth of truth from our lives ought to have two things. What are those two things? Explain the significance of each one.
    A. _____
    B. _____
    C. Read I Timothy 6:17-18. This all translates into the fact that we are not intended to be *treasure chests* for truth, but _____ centers.

4. If you *possess* wisdom, does that automatically make you a wise person? What is it that makes you a wise person?

5. What is the emphasis in teaching wisdom to others?

6. Do the "psalms and hymns and spiritual songs" refer to songs in our hymnals or songs written by contemporary writers?
    A. What is the believer being challenged to do here?
    B. How does the truth of Matthew 6:19-21 help us grasp the meaning of this?

7. What is the meaning of the words "with grace in your hearts"?
    A. If music is intended for worship, what must be its focus?
    B. Can true praise be manufactured?
    C. Where does true praise come from?

8. As Christians, on whom does everything we do in this world reflect? How is your reflection?

Jesus is Lord!

Studies in the Epistle to the Colossians
Chapter Eighteen
ROLE MODELING CHRISTIANITY
THROUGH RELATIONSHIPS

"[18] Wives, submit yourselves unto your own husbands, as it is fit in the Lord. [19] Husbands, love *your* wives, and be not bitter against them. [20] Children, obey *your* parents in all things: for this is well pleasing unto the Lord. [21] Fathers, provoke not your children *to anger*, lest they be discouraged. [22] Servants, obey in all things *your* masters according to the flesh; not with eyeservice, as menpleasers; but in singleness of heart, fearing God: [23] And whatsoever ye do, do *it* heartily, as to the Lord, and not unto men; [24] Knowing that of the Lord ye shall receive the reward of the inheritance: for ye serve the Lord Christ. [25] But he that doeth wrong shall receive for the wrong which he hath done: and there is no respect of persons. [1] Masters, give unto *your* servants that which is just and equal; knowing that ye also have a Master in heaven" (Colossians 3:18-4:1).

When Jesus is Lord of our relationships, those relationships fall under at least one (usually more) of four authorities. Yet, we must constantly remind ourselves that all of these relationships fall under the Lordship of Christ. We can never be submissive to our supreme Authority (Jesus) if we refuse to be submissive to any one of God's other four ordained authorities.

In Colossians 3:18-25, we move from a general exhortation to specifics regarding these relationships. God wants us to understand that, although we are all positionally equal in Christ as believers, we still have individual responsibilities and functions in life. These are called ROLES. Each role has its own distinctions. Some of these roles are wives, husbands, children, fathers, mothers, "servants" (employees), and "masters" (employers).

The distinctions between these roles pertain to

God's commands defining how each role relates to the other roles. The distinctions describe individual responsibilities to one another in various relationships. The believer who accepts the Lordship of Jesus over his life also accepts his responsibilities in these various relationships. In doing so, he submits to the Lord's commands for each. "Submitting yourselves one to another in the fear of God" (Ephesians 5:21).

THE FIRST ROLE GIVEN IS TO THE WIFE.
"Wives, submit yourselves unto your own husbands, as it is fit (right) in the Lord" (Colossians 3:18).

The distinction "wife" refers to how she is to relate to her husband (not to anyone else). "Wife" describes the relationship. A wife is not a wife if she does not fulfill her distinction. The command (distinction) for her relationship to her husband is to "submit."

The word "submit" is from the Greek word *hupotasso* (hoop-ot-as'-so). It means (1) to arrange under, to subordinate; (2) to subject, put in subjection; (3) to subject one's self, obey; (4) to submit to one's control; (5) to yield to one's admonition or advice; (6) to obey, be subject.

Hupotasso is a Greek military term meaning to arrange troop divisions in a military fashion under the command of a leader. In non-military use, it was a voluntary attitude of giving in, cooperating, assuming responsibility, and carrying a burden.

The degree of a wife's submission to her husband is the same degree expected of all believers as they submit to the Lord Jesus.

"[22] Wives, submit yourselves unto your own husbands, <u>as unto the Lord</u>. [23] For the husband is the head of the wife, even as Christ is the head of the church: and he is the saviour of the body. [24] Therefore as the church is subject unto Christ, so let the wives be to their own husbands in every thing" (Ephesians 5:22-24).

The wife does not submit to her husband because he is superior to her. She submits because Jesus is Lord and

148

He commands her to submit to her husband. The wife that fails to do what Jesus commands is living in sin.

What is the Lord's purpose in commanding the wife to submit to her husband? A wife's submission to her husband provides order in that relationship.

"For God is not the author of confusion, but of peace, as in all churches of the saints" (I Corinthians 14:33).

Her voluntary submission to her husband is a role model for the voluntary submission of her children to the Lordship of Christ. In homes, where the wife is not submissive to the husband (in the Lord), the children's understanding of submission to the Lordship of Christ is usually destroyed. This has been one of the greatest damages done by *Women's Lib* to the family. Rebellion breeds more rebellion. In Colossians 3:18, the words "as it is fit in the Lord" emphasize a moral obligation. The wife should portray to her husband, to her children, and the world this voluntary submission to her husband, because it is her moral obligation.

THE SECOND ROLE GIVEN IS THE HUSBAND
"Husbands, love your wives, and be not bitter against them" (Colossians 3:19).

The distinction of the word "husband" refers to how he is to relate to his wife. "Husband" describes the relationship. A husband is not a husband if he does not fulfill his distinction. The husband has two commands (distinctions) for his relationship to his wife.

1. The first command is to "love" his wife. The word "love" is from the Greek word *agapao* (ag-ap-ah'-o). When used in regard to other people, it means to welcome, to entertain, to be fond of, and to love dearly. The responsibility attached to the word is that of self-sacrifice for the benefit of another.

"Husbands, love your wives, even as Christ also loved the church, and gave himself for it" (Ephesians 5:25).

2. The second command is "be not bitter against them."

149

The word "bitter" is from the Greek word *pikraino* (pik-rah'-ee-no). It means to "(1) embitter, exasperate; (2) render angry, indignant; (3) to be embittered, irritated; (4) to visit with bitterness, to grieve (deal bitterly with)." The husband should not only to be willing to make extreme sacrifices for his wife, but also be tender and appreciative.

What is the Lord's purpose in these two commands to the husband? These two commands teach what Jesus means by the word "love" - the willingness to give sacrificially of ourselves to another. They teach the need to be gentle with people. These two commands are some of the first things children need to learn. Before they learn to communicate verbally, these truths need to be continually *role modeled* before them. Therefore, the father in a home teaches his children how to love the Lord and others.

THE THIRD ROLE GIVEN IS THE CHILDREN
"Children, obey your parents in all things: for this is well pleasing unto the Lord" (Colossians 3:20).

The distinction "children" refers to how children are to relate to their parents (the husband and wife). The word "children" describes the relationship (not the age). The child's command is "obey." The word "obey" is from the Greek word *hupakouo* (hoop-ak-oo'-o). It means to "(1) to listen, to harken; (2) of one who on the knock at the door comes to listen who it is; (the duty of a porter); (3) to harken to a command; or (4) to obey, be obedient to, submit to."

Children **learn** obedience. The first way they do so is through the *role modeling* of parents. In Ephesians 6:1-2, children are given a second command.

"[1] Children, obey your parents in the Lord: for this is right. [2] Honour thy father and mother; (which is the first commandment with promise)."

The word "honor" is from the Greek word *timao* (tim-ah'-o). It means "(1) to estimate, fix the value, (2) for the value of something belonging to one's self, (3) to honour, to have in honour, to revere, venerate." This means that the child is to evaluate the divinely appointed position of the authority of parents and treat them with reverence, courtesy, respect, and obedience. Obedience is the duty that finds its motivation in the proper biblical evaluation of another person's position ("honor").

Why are children to be taught to obey and honor their parents? Children who are not taught these things about their parents will not know that they are responsible to obey and honor the Lord. Since children have difficulty understanding abstract concepts such as submission, obedience, honor, and love to an invisible God, their training must be in concrete realities. When these commands are learned about parents in the physical world, they can be applied spiritually to God while living in the physical world.

THE FOURTH ROLE GIVEN IS FOR CHRISTIAN EMPLOYEES

"**[22] Servants, obey in all things your masters according to the flesh; not with eyeservice, as menpleasers; but in singleness of heart, fearing God: [23] And whatsoever ye do, do it heartily, as to the Lord, and not unto men; [24] Knowing that of the Lord ye shall receive the reward of the inheritance: for ye serve the Lord Christ**" (Colossians 3:22-24).

The distinction is how the employee relates to his employer. The command "obey" comes with definitive qualifications. "Obey" is from the same Greek word used for children in their relationship with their parents. There are some definitive qualifications of that obedience.

1. "Not with eyeservice" - this means obedience ought not to be something done for an outward show.
2. "Singleness of heart . . . as to the Lord" - obedience should be from the *heart* as if serving God the Father or the Lord Jesus Christ. The word "heart" refers to the motivation/attitude of obedience.
3. "Heartily" - Christians ought to work for their employer with the same zeal and spirit they give to the Lord.

4. "For ye serve the Lord Christ" - Christians should view everything they do as unto the Lord, not for men.

Why should the Christian employee serve in this way?

1. The Christian employee should be an example of the most loyal, humble, submissive, and concerned person in the work force.

2. The Christian employee should live before the world as a person who recognizes his accountability to God in every avenue of his life.

3. The over ruling principle has already been stated in Colossians 3:17.

"And whatsoever ye do in word or deed, do all in the name of the Lord Jesus, giving thanks to God and the Father by him."

THE FIFTH ROLE GIVEN IS FOR CHRISTIAN EMPLOYERS
"Masters, give unto your servants that which is just and equal; knowing that ye also have a Master in heaven" (Colossians 4:1).

The distinction is how the employer relates to his employees. The command is to be "just and equal" with them. The word "just" is from the Greek word *dikaios* (dik'-ah-yos). In this context it means rendering to each his due and that in a judicial sense, passing just judgment on others, whether expressed in words or shown by the manner of dealing with them. The word "equal" is from the Greek word *isotes* (e-sot'-ace). It means (1) equality, or (2) equity, fairness, what is equitable.

Why should the Christian employer treat his employees justly and fairly? The Christian employer treat his employees justly and fairly because every Christian should publicly and privately exemplify these character traits by always dealing with people according to what is biblically right. He should also always deal with people fairly. Man's natural tendency is to make all decisions with prejudice towards those he favors and against those he disfavors. God wants *equitability*. God is not a respecter of persons.

> "Then Peter opened his mouth, and said, Of a truth I perceive that God is no respecter of persons" (Acts 10:34).

God has defined these relationships to provide order in a fallen world. The Christian who has submitted to the Lordship of Christ will work in each of these relationships according to these role models as God defines them. How are you role modeling Christ in your marriage, family, or work?

Jesus is Lord!

Studies in the Epistle to the Colossians
Chapter Eighteen
ROLE MODELING CHRISTIANITY
THROUGH RELATIONSHIPS

1. Read Colossians 3:18. What is the first role given?
   A. To what does the distinction "wife" refer?
   B. What is the command that defines her distinction?
   C. What do you think is the Lord's purpose in commanding the wife to do this?

2. Read Colossians 3:19. What is the second role given?
   A. To what does the distinction "husband" refer?
   B. What are the two commands that define his distinction?
   C. What do you think is the Lord's purpose in commanding the husband to do this?

3. Read Colossians 3:20. What is the third role given?
   A. To what does the distinction "children" refer?
   C. What do you think is the Lord's purpose in commanding the child to do this?
   D. How do children **learn** obedience?

4. Read Colossians 3:22-24. What is the fourth role given?
   A. To what does the distinction "servant" refer?
   B. What is the command that defines this distinction?
   C. What do you think is the Lord's purpose in commanding the "servant" to do this?
   D. What verse in Colossians has already stated the overall governing principle for this role model?
   E. Give the definitive qualifications of how the command is to be fulfilled.

5. Read Colossians 4:1. What is the fifth role given?
   A. To what does the distinction "master" refer?
   B. What two words define this distinction?
   C. What do you think is the Lord's purpose in commanding the "master" to do this?

   Evaluate your roles in the various relationships that apply to you. Is there an area of your life that needs to be corrected to correspond with these roles? Define what needs

to be done and set some goals to accomplish this. **Begin by confessing your failure to others in these relationships to which you have been a poor role model. Until you fulfill your responsibilities in these relationships, you are living in sin.**

"For rebellion *is as* the sin of witchcraft, and stubbornness *is as* iniquity and idolatry. Because thou hast rejected the word of the LORD, he hath also rejected thee from *being* king" (I Samuel 15:23).

Jesus is Lord!

Studies in the Epistle to the Colossians
Chapter Nineteen
NORMALITIES AND ABNORMALITIES
OF CHRISTIAN RELATIONSHIPS
IN MARRIAGE AND SINGLENESS

"[16] Let the word of Christ dwell in you richly in all wisdom; teaching and admonishing one another in psalms and hymns and spiritual songs, singing with grace in your hearts to the Lord. [17] And whatsoever ye do in word or deed, *do* all in the name of the Lord Jesus, giving thanks to God and the Father by him. [18] Wives, submit yourselves unto your own husbands, as it is fit in the Lord. [19] Husbands, love *your* wives, and be not bitter against them. [20] Children, obey *your* parents in all things: for this is well pleasing unto the Lord. [21] Fathers, provoke not your children *to anger*, lest they be discouraged" (Colossians 3:16-21).

COLOSSIANS 3:16-21 GIVES THE FOUNDATIONAL TRUTHS FOR *NORMAL* CHRISTIAN RELATIONSHIPS. NORMAL MEANS THE HIGHEST STANDARD.

There are foundational truths for the wife to have a normal relationship with her husband (Colossians 3:18; compare Ephesians 5:22-24). Submission teaches lordship. It is the normal (God-ordained) responsibility of the wife in the family to be in submission to her husband thereby teaching lordship to her family, children, and world.

"[22] Wives, submit yourselves unto your own husbands, as unto the Lord. [23] For the husband is the head of the wife, even as Christ is the head of the church: and he is the saviour of the body. [24] Therefore as the church is subject unto Christ, so let the wives be to their own husbands in every thing" (Ephesians 5:22-24).

There are foundational truths for the husband to have a normal relationship with his wife (Colossians 3:19; compare Ephesians 5:25-29).

156

"²⁵ Husbands, love your wives, even as Christ also loved the church, and gave himself for it; ²⁶ That he might sanctify and cleanse it with the washing of water by the word, ²⁷ That he might present it to himself a glorious church, not having spot, or wrinkle, or any such thing; but that it should be holy and without blemish. ²⁸ So ought men to love their wives as their own bodies. He that loveth his wife loveth himself. ²⁹ For no man ever yet hated his own flesh; but nourisheth and cherisheth it, even as the Lord the church" (Ephesians 5:25-29).

The word "love" means the extreme of self-sacrifice. It is the normal (God-ordained) responsibility of the husband in the family situation to sacrifice his own personal desires in order to meet the needs of his wife and family. He thereby teaches and establishes the principal of self-sacrifice and teaches his family to love others biblically.

There are foundational truths for children to have a normal relationship with their parents (Colossians 3:20; compare Ephesians 6:1-3).

"¹ Children, obey your parents in the Lord: for this is right. ² Honour thy father and mother; (which is the first commandment with promise;) ³ That it may be well with thee, and thou mayest live long on the earth" (Ephesians 6:1-3).

Obedience and honor are two central essences of worship. They flow naturally from the established attributes of submission and self-sacrifice. The opposites are rebellion and selfishness. Therefore, the God-ordained norm for children is for them to possess the attributes taught them in the normal (God-ordained) marriage relationship of submission and self-sacrifice. When these are established, they will result in the proper character traits of honor and obedience. In turn this will result in children who find it the norm, rather than the abnorm, to submit to Jesus Christ as Lord, to be governed by His Word and to honor and obey Him in every aspect of life. The goal is the continual worship and praise of God, not just in *lip service*, but in *life service*.

If the norm is not realized, the abnorm will result. Wives who do not submit will produce rebellious children. An example is the effect of *Women's Lib* has had on society. Husbands who do not practice self-sacrificing will produce selfish children. Suicide is the epitome of selfishness. It is the highest among teenagers today. Suicide is not a cry for help as much as it is a cry for order and absolutes.

GOD'S NORM FOR MARRIAGE
(NORM MEANS THE GOD-ORDAINED IDEAL)

"[4] And he answered and said unto them, Have ye not read, that he which made them at the beginning made them male and female, [5] And said, For this cause shall a man leave father and mother, and shall cleave to his wife: and they twain shall be one flesh? [6] Wherefore they are no more twain, but one flesh. What therefore God hath joined together, let not man put asunder" (Matthew 19:4-6).

Man and woman were specially **designed** for each other. In marriage, God actually unites two people spiritually as one.

"Therefore shall a man leave his father and his mother, and shall cleave unto his wife: and they shall be one flesh" (Genesis 2:24).

"[6] But from the beginning of the creation God made them male and female. [7] For this cause shall a man leave his father and mother, and cleave to his wife; [8] And they twain shall be one flesh: so then they are no more twain, but one flesh. [9] What therefore God hath joined together, let not man put asunder" (Mark 10:6-9).

Marriage is intended to be monogamous. Mark 10:7 does not say *to his wives*. Mark 10:8 does not say *they three or four shall be one flesh*. Marriage is intended to be an unbroken partnership. In a partnership, partners do not do the same things. They use their individual qualities to compliment what the other lacks. They complete each other. Example: it is a fact of social behavior that men make decisions based upon fact more than emotions. The opposite is true of women.

Marriage is for this life only. "For in the resurrection they neither marry, nor are given in marriage, but are as the angels of God in heaven" (Matthew 22:30). This verse contradicts Mormon beliefs. Mark 12:25 and Luke 20:35 are verses stating this same thing are.

"For when they shall rise from the dead, they neither marry, nor are given in marriage; but are as the angels which are in heaven" (Mark 12:25).

"But they which shall be accounted worthy to obtain that world, and the resurrection from the dead, neither marry, nor are given in marriage" (Luke 20:35).

Anytime a proclaimed *new revelation* (such as the Book of Mormon) contradicts *old revelation*, throw out the new in its totality.

"[32] And the spirits of the prophets are subject to the prophets. [33] For God is not the author of confusion, but of peace, as in all churches of the saints" (I Corinthians. 14:32-33).

Any new prophecy is subject to evaluation as to its truth by comparison to the established truth of the established prophets (I Corinthians 14:32). God is not the author of confusion. He is consistent in truth (I Corinthians 14:33).

AVOIDING MARRIAGE ABNORMALITIES

Because relationships are based upon social interaction, or more aptly social inter-reaction, the norm is only realized when all parties understand and are in compliance to absolute biblical principles. When this is not realized, abnormal relationships result. This happens when people do not practically apply the ideals of God for their lives. They are not equally "transformed by the renewing of their minds." They don't grow at the same levels. They are not equally yielded to the Spirit of God.

BIBLICAL PRINCIPLES FOR ELIMINATING ABNORMALITIES IN MARRIAGES AND OTHER RELATIONSHIPS

"Be ye not unequally yoked together with unbelievers: for what fellowship hath righteousness with unrighteousness? and what communion hath light with darkness" (II Corinthians 6:14).

What is an "unbeliever"? The word comes from the Greek word *apistos* (ap'-is-tos). It means to be unfaithful or faithless, (not to be trusted, perfidious), incredible, unbelieving, incredulous, without trust (in God).

This first and primary principal establishes that salvation is not all that is necessary for the foundation of a relationship. Just as in the church, co-operation with others is not determined by a testimony of faith in Christ, but by the exhibition of faithfulness to Christ by obedience to His Word. So it should be in choosing a husband or wife. It is not enough to have the same God. Couples must have the same Lord.

Can Jesus be Lord if we say we have faith in the Word of God as a governing force of life and we do not live accordingly? Couples need to test each other before they are married to see if both are truly believers in the same sense.

"[1] Beloved, believe not every spirit, but try the spirits whether they are of God: because many false prophets are gone out into the world. [2] Hereby know ye the Spirit of God: Every spirit that confesseth that Jesus Christ is come in the flesh is of God: [3] And every spirit that confesseth not that Jesus Christ is come in the flesh is not of God: and this is that spirit of antichrist, whereof ye have heard that it should come; and even now already is it in the world. [4] Ye are of God, little children, and have overcome them: because greater is he that is in you, than he that is in the world. [5] They are of the world: therefore speak they of the world, and the world heareth them. [6] We are of God: he that knoweth God heareth us; he that is not of God heareth not us. Hereby know we the spirit of truth, and the spirit of error" (I John 4:1-6).

I John 4:5 gives us a test for those who profess Christ, but do not allow Him to be Lord. They will be preoccupied with the things of the world, rather than Christ. I John 4:6 is another test. If they are God's, they hear

God's Word. The word "hear" in this context means to listen with the intention of obeying what is heard. This is the testing ground for genuineness or pretense. To hear God's Word without being intent on obeying it is self-deception regarding the Lordship of Christ.

> "[21] Wherefore lay apart all filthiness and superfluity of naughtiness, and receive with meekness the engrafted word, which is able to save your souls. [22] But be ye doers of the word, and not hearers only, deceiving your own selves" (James 1:21-22).

The overlying principle in all this is that couples should hold to the same *belief system*. *Belief systems* are beliefs that govern life and its practices. If couples have different *belief systems*, they may profess to have the same God, but they will have different Lords.

The Lordship of Jesus centers on people following His teachings. If a couple disagrees on the meaning of those teachings, they will not be able to walk together through life. There will be constant conflict and the need for continual compromise. The Lord knows what He is talking about when He asks the question, "Can two walk together, except they be agreed" (Amos 3:3)?

It is imperative for couples to work at growing together spiritually. If they do not grow together, they will soon be growing apart. Couples not growing together will be two lives going in two separate directions, but heading for the same destiny - FAILURE!

Jesus is Lord!

Studies in the Epistle to the Colossians
Chapter Nineteen
NORMALITIES AND ABNORMALITIES
OF CHRISTIAN RELATIONSHIPS
IN MARRIAGE AND SINGLENESS

1. What does the word *normal* mean from a biblical context?

   A. What is the word that describes a wife's *normal* relationship with her husband?

   B. What is the word that describes a husband's *normal* relationship with his wife?

   C. What are the two words that describe a child's *normal* relationship with his parents?

2. Read Matthew 19:4-6. What are some of the biblical *norms* (ideals) for marriage?

   A. Men and women are _____ for each other

   B. Marriage is intended to be mon_____.
(The answer is not: monotonous.)

   C. Marriage is intended to be an _____ relationship.

3. Will marriages continue after death and resurrection?

4. Besides the obvious physical things, what is another way God has designed men and women differently so that they can complete each other?

5. What happens when couples fail to spiritually grow at to same levels of walk with the Lord?

6. Read I Corinthians 6:14. From your understanding of the Greek word translated "unbeliever," can a believer ever be an unbeliever as well?

   A. What principle should courting couples apply from this?

   B. How can a couple profess to believe in the same God, but have different Lords?

Jesus is Lord!

Studies in the Epistle to the Colossians

Chapter Twenty

DEALING SCRIPTURALLY WITH ABNORMAL MARRIAGE RELATIONSHIPS

"[10] And unto the married I command, yet not I, but the Lord, Let not the wife depart from her husband: [11] But and if she depart, let her remain unmarried, or be reconciled to her husband: and let not the husband put away his wife. [12] But to the rest speak I, not the Lord: If any brother hath a wife that believeth not, and she be pleased to dwell with him, let him not put her away. [13] And the woman which hath an husband that believeth not, and if he be pleased to dwell with her, let her not leave him. [14] For the unbelieving husband is sanctified by the wife, and the unbelieving wife is sanctified by the husband: else were your children unclean; but now are they holy. [15] But if the unbelieving depart, let him depart. A brother or a sister is not under bondage in such cases: but God hath called us to peace. [16] For what knowest thou, O wife, whether thou shalt save thy husband? or how knowest thou, O man, whether thou shalt save thy wife? [17] But as God hath distributed to every man, as the Lord hath called every one, so let him walk. And so ordain I in all churches" (I Corinthians 7:10-17).

THERE WERE FOUR DIFFERENT KINDS OF MARRIAGES IN THE ROMAN EMPIRE AT THE TIME OF THE WRITING OF SCRIPTURE. Local churches would have to deal with these abnormalities throughout the Church Age.

1. THE FIRST WAS THE CONTUBERNIUM. This means *tent companionship*. These were slaves that were allowed to live together by their owners. Many of the early Christians were slaves. Their marriages were abnormalities existing before their salvation and carried into their post-salvation lives. These relationships greatly affected their being able to live for Christ and allow Him to be Lord of their homes. Because of these difficulties, the Corinthian believers wondered if they should end these abnormal pre-salvation marriages to unbelievers. Through the Apostle Paul, God gives clear revelation to the Christian's responsibility in these abnormal situations (see vs. 10-12).

I Corinthians 7:12 is new revelation coming through the Apostle Paul that had not previously been addressed by Jesus before His ascension. This does not mean it is not inspired of God. Regardless the degree of social acceptance of the abnorm, it never becomes the norm simply because the abnorm is the majority. God's Word always determines what is normal.

2. THE SECOND TYPE OF MARRIAGE WAS THE USUS. This was marriage between the *common people* of the Roman culture. This type was the majority of Gentile marriages. It was known as *common-law marriage*. If a man or woman lived together for one year, at the end of that year they became identified as husband and wife. The church would have to biblically correct and deal with such relationships.

3. THE THIRD TYPE OF MARRIAGE WAS COEMTIO IN MANUM (*marriage by sale*). This existed in two forms. The first was more of a breeding arrangement between pagan slave owners. Usually, these were short term arrangements for the purpose of producing off-spring. Until surrogate motherhood entered our culture, we would have never thought the modern church would have to deal with this kind of relationship. The second form of this type of marriage was when a father would sell a daughter for marriage. Female children were a commodity in many cultures. It is still done in some cultures today.

4. THE FOURTH TYPE OF MARRIAGE WAS THE CONFARREATIO. These were sophisticated marriages of the noble families of the Roman Empire involving elaborate ceremonies of opulent wealth. Each would try to outdo the other. Most of modern wedding customs come from pagan Rome. Some of these customs were elaborate cakes, meals, and celebrations with music and dancing. The bride wore expensive gowns, had wreaths, and surrounded herself with flowers.

Because a second century Roman writer (Auless Gelling, *Gellius 10.10*) stated the third finger of the left hand had a nerve running to the heart, it became the custom of placing a ring on that finger. People putting on these elaborate shows today aren't *keeping up with the Jones*. They are keeping up with the pagan Romans.

Local churches were filled with saved people who had all these types of marriage backgrounds. These relationships and marriages would have to be re-established on biblical foundations. The problem was that the culture was in opposition to doctrine (truth). The world was in opposition to the Lordship of Christ.

The doctrinal answer to a problem of such a complex cultural abnormality was the Scriptural teaching of the sanctity of marriage regardless of its form. Believers were to function within their situation correcting what they could when they could. This does not condone entering into such an abnormal and unscriptural union. Nor does it condone correcting the abnormality through divorce. Two abnormalities do not make something normal (*two wrongs don't make a right*).

SCRIPTURALLY DEALING WITH THESE TYPES OF ABNORMALITIES

There was a social chaos in the Roman Empire (causing great stress on relationships) which resulted in a proportionate increase in the divorce rate. Chaos comes from confusion in circumstances due to the loss of absolute norms. Without absolutes there is no way to determine what normal behavior is. If there is no such thing as normal behavior, there can be no such thing as right or wrong behavior. If there is no such thing as right or wrong behavior, there can be no right or wrong response to behavior.

Due to this social chaos, divorce became so socially acceptable that some people were married over twenty times. William Barclay notes an historical document where a woman was getting married for her twenty-seventh time to a man who was going to be married for his twenty-sixth time. The only way to restore order to this type of society is to restore absolute norms.

"[16] All scripture is given by inspiration of God, and is profitable for doctrine, for reproof, for correction, for instruction in righteousness: [17] That the man of God may be perfect, thoroughly furnished unto all good works" (II Timothy 3:16-17).

HISTORICAL FACTORS CONTRIBUTING TO A HIGH DIVORCE RATE ONCE ABSOLUTES ARE REMOVED

1. Homosexuality
2. Polygamy
3. Concubines (household prostitutes)
4. Women's liberation movement

Women's Lib is nothing new. In the Roman Empire women entered into competition with men in every arena. The Roman society ridiculed the women who would not compete, calling them weak and useless. Women even entered into competitive feats of strength with men in the sports. Women also became the sexual aggressors of their society. This confused the roles so badly that homosexuality increased.

THERE ARE TWO MAJOR SOCIAL ABNORMALITIES PERPETUATING PROGRESSIVE ABNORMALITIES COMING FROM REMOVED ABSOLUTES. EACH OF THESE WILL INCREASE TO THE DEGREE THAT ABNORMS ARE CONSIDERED NORMAL.

1. Sexual immorality and perversion
2. Violence and crime

All sexual abnormalities can be directly related to the abolition of biblical absolutes (read I Corinthians 6:12-18). For the people at Corinth, sex was only a biological function (*this is the philosophy of present public sex education*). Without biblical absolutes, people look at sex as if it is amoral. Without biblical absolutes, it is neither wrong nor right to have sexual relations outside of a husband/wife relationship. It is like blowing your nose, if it needs to be done, then do it. Without biblical absolutes, there can be no sexual behavior considered abnormal or deviant, resulting in alternative choices to heterosexual relationships.

The name Corinth was a descriptive word relating the nature of this culture. *Korinthiazestha* is the Greek word that Corinthia comes from. It means to live in drunken and immoral debauchery.

The Church at Corinth had divorced their moral responsibility from salvation and law (absolutes) from grace. They had allowed their society to influence and distort their understanding of God's absolutes. Instead of being the positive example of what a society can be when the absolutes of God's Word are accepted, they were little more than a step behind their culture.

The church that wants to influence a society with moral law when it is not even willing to do so in its own miniature is a farce. How can a church expect a society to adopt its absolutes, when they don't believe them enough to practice them in their smaller community (the local church)? How can a church tell a society not to hate and kill when their own community cannot even love one another?

Every local church is an ongoing social example of their testimony of faith in God's absolutes and a model for all cultures/societies. When a church begins to live those absolutes in their everyday lives, they testify they believe these absolutes work. When they refuse to live by those absolutes, they are a living testimony to their world that the absolutes of God do not work. When that happens, they are telling everyone it is not important to allow Jesus to be Lord of our lives. He can be Savior, but not Lord. We can trust His Word for salvation, but apparently for little else. What a sad testimony for the Lordship of Christ!

Jesus is Lord!

Studies in the Epistle to the Colossians
Chapter Twenty
DEALING SCRIPTURALLY WITH ABNORMAL MARRIAGE RELATIONSHIPS

1. From the following list of the four types of marriages at the time of the writing of the New Testament, discuss how each should be dealt with Scripturally.
   A. CONTUBERNIUM:
   B. USUS:
   C. COEMTIO IN MANUM:
   D. CONFARREATIO:

2. Were all of these types of marriage relationships supposed to be honored by Christians according to Paul in I Corinthians 7:10-16?

3. Read I Corinthians 7:12. Was Paul saying that this statement was not inspired of God? What is he saying?

4. Even when abnormal things are accepted by society as normal, what is the only way to really determine what is normal?
   A. Do you think you measure everything according to that standard?
   B. Can you think of anything you may not be measuring according to that standard that needs to be?

5. Read I Corinthians 7:17. Since the context is one of dealing with abnormal marriage relationships, apply this instruction to the believer's responsibility in that abnormal relationship. What should be his immediate goal and long term goal in that relationship?

6. To what can the chaos of abnormal relationships be traced in any society?

7. Read II Timothy 3:16-17. What is the only way to restore order to a society in chaos?

8. What are two progressive abnormalities that will increase proportionately to the degree a society moves away from biblical absolutes?

Jesus is Lord!

Studies in the Epistle to the Colossians
Chapter Twenty-one
PUTTING SPIRITUAL FLESH ON OUR THEOLOGICAL BONES
(Living the Truth We Know)

"[2] Continue in prayer, and watch in the same with thanksgiving; [3] Withal praying also for us, that God would open unto us a door of utterance, to speak the mystery of Christ, for which I am also in bonds: [4] That I may make it manifest, as I ought to speak. [5] Walk in wisdom toward them that are without, redeeming the time. [6] Let your speech be alway with grace, seasoned with salt, that ye may know how ye ought to answer every man" (Colossians 4:2-6).

It is important to note that Colossians 4:1 should actually be part of chapter three and 4:2 should be the beginning of chapter four. If we do not see the break here, the instruction of 4:2-6 would be understood to be to the "masters" of 4:1. This is obviously not the intention. This is intended for all believers.

The first part of the epistle to the Colossians establishes the doctrine of the Lordship of Christ. Chapter 3:1 through 4:1 shows us how to live the Lordship of Christ in our relationships. Chapter 4:2-6 commands the believer to minister the Lordship of Christ to others through two avenues. The believer is to pray for other believers (vs. 2-3) and live and communicate to the lost (vs. 4-6).

CONTINUE PRAYING
(Colossians 4:2)

Prayer is an area of ministry that many Christians do not understand. Prayer is as much an attitude as it is something we do. Prayer is living continually in conscious awareness of God's presence and dependency upon Him. The attitude of prayer is an unbroken line of communication between the believer and his Lord. The admonition to continue in prayer is one of maintaining that unbroken line of *moment by moment* communication and dependency. The primary focus of maintaining "fellowship" (synergism) with God is to keep the lines of communication open. The flow of God's power to our lives as Christians flows through that same line.

PEOPLE OF PRAYER EXPECT GOD TO ACT.
"Watch in the same with thanksgiving" (Colossians 4:2).

The word "watch" in Colossians 4:2 is from the Greek *gregoreuo* (gray-gor-yoo'-o). It means to watch for something to happen or to come. Metaphorically it means to give strict attention to something, be cautious, active, to take heed lest through remission and indolence some destructive calamity might suddenly overtake you.

Those that understand the spiritual dynamic of prayer expect both God's response and Satan's opposition to that response. Prayer enters us onto the battlefield of spiritual warfare and into the *battle of the ages* for the souls of mankind. Prayer is serious business for serious people of God. We are powerless in the battle without the synergism that comes from yielding our bodies to the Lord (consecration) in holiness (sanctification). Prayer should never be something we enter into without first putting on our spiritual armor.

> "Praying always with all prayer and supplication in the Spirit, and watching thereunto with all perseverance and supplication for all saints" (Ephesians 6:18).

> "But the end of all things is at hand: be ye therefore sober, and watch unto prayer" (I Peter 4:7).

If watchfulness is the *attention* of prayer, thanksgiving is the *intention* of prayer. The believer should live in constant praise and thanksgiving to God, because of continual access to His throne of grace in the Lord Jesus Christ. How easily we forget that without Christ as the High Priest, Advocate, and Mediator between God and man, we would have no access to God in prayer.

"[14] Seeing then that we have a great high priest, that is

170

passed into the heavens, Jesus the Son of God, let us hold fast our profession. [15] For we have not an high priest which cannot be touched with the feeling of our infirmities; but was in all points tempted like as we are, yet without sin. [16] Let us therefore come boldly unto the throne of grace, that we may obtain mercy, and find grace to help in time of need" (Hebrews 4:14-16).

THE COMMUNITY IN PRAYER
"Withal praying also for us" (Colossians 4:3)

The word "withal" is translated from the Greek word *hama* (ham'-ah). It means *at the same time, at once,* and *together with others.* It refers to the synergism of prayer. Prayer should be a central occupation in the assembling and communion of a local church. The prayer life of every local church and every Christian should be focused prayer (*targeted*).

The focus of the communal prayer life of a local church is for open doors of opportunity for individual believers to preach the Gospel publicly and privately to lost people. Targeted prayer takes two main directions. When the church gathers to pray, they should be praying for the lost and for each other to have opportunities to tell the lost of Christ and how to be saved. We need to pray for one another so that when God opens a door of opportunity, we will be spiritually aware of it and have the boldness to present the Gospel.

Prayer for other believers should also be focused on their being enabled of God to give the Gospel to the lost so that the lost might see their need and Christ's provision (4:4). The primary aspect of this prayer life for one another is that we can maintain unbroken "fellowship" with God individually and corporately. We are to maintain unbroken fellowship with God so that the dynamic of the spiritual synergism of the local church remains intact. Then the "power" of God (II Timothy 3:5) abides in us as we abide in Christ (John 15:1-3).

The believer must be able to present the Gospel with clarity. This requires the leading of the Holy Spirit, the convincing of the Holy Spirit, the illumination of the

Holy Spirit, and the empowering/enabling grace of the Holy Spirit (synergism).

> "But sanctify the Lord God in your hearts: and be ready always to give an answer to every man that asketh you a reason of the hope that is in you with meekness and fear" (I Peter 3:15).

> "Study to shew thyself approved unto God, a workman that needeth not to be ashamed, rightly dividing the word of truth" (II Timothy 2:15).

The lost must receive the Gospel with understanding. Notice how many times the Lord emphasizes the essential of <u>understanding</u> in the parable from Matthew chapter thirteen before anyone can be "converted."

> "For this people's heart is waxed gross, and their ears are dull of hearing, and their eyes they have closed; lest at any time they should see with their eyes, and hear with their ears, and should <u>understand</u> with their heart, and should <u>be converted</u>, and I should heal them" (Matthew 13:15).

> "[18] Hear ye therefore the parable of the sower. [19] When any one heareth the word of the kingdom, and <u>understandeth it not</u>, then cometh the wicked one, and catcheth away that which was sown in his heart. This is he which received seed by the way side. [20] But he that received the seed into stony places, the same is he that heareth the word, and anon with joy receiveth it; [21] Yet hath he not root in himself, but dureth for a while: for when tribulation or persecution ariseth because of the word, by and by he is offended. [22] He also that received seed among the thorns is he that heareth the word; and the care of this world, and the deceitfulness of riches, choke the word, and he becometh unfruitful. [23] But he that received seed into the good ground is he that heareth the word, <u>and understandeth it</u>; which also beareth fruit, and bringeth forth, some an hundredfold, some sixty, some thirty" (Matthew 13:18-23).

IN COLOSSIANS 4:5, THE FOCUS MOVES AWAY FROM THOSE WITHIN THE LOCAL CHURCH TO THOSE OUTSIDE ("WITHOUT").

Just as the Lordship of Christ defines certain responsibilities of believers to one another, His Lordship gives specific instruction on how to live before and among the lost.

FIRST, WE ARE TO "WALK IN WISDOM TOWARD THEM."

The word "walk" is from the Greek word *peripateo* (per-ee-pat-eh'-o). It means to *make due use of opportunities*. It means to *regulate one's life or to conduct one's self in a certain way*. That *way* is defined by the word "wisdom." In the context of this verse, this means to live devoutly with proper prudence in relationships with lost people who are not disciples of Christ. It also means having skill and discretion in imparting truth to them. It also means having the knowledge and practice of the requisites for godly and upright living before them.

SECONDLY, WE ARE TO REDEEM TIME.

In other words, don't waste time. Use it wisely and for the furtherance of the cause of Christ. Time is not an endless commodity. Wasted time is usually wasted opportunity.

THIRDLY, WHAT WE SAY TO THE LOST SHOULD BE PREOCCUPIED "WITH" THE GRACE OF GOD UPON OUR LIVES AND AVAILABLE TO THEM.

The grace of God refers to the divine empowering of the believer's service gifts as defined in Romans 12:1-8. This emphasis on "grace" is an emphasis on the synergism that results when the trichotomy of a believer is completely yielded to God's will (Romans 6:11-13). The epistle to the Ephesians church is an example of speech preoccupied with the grace of God. Look at a few selected verses through this epistle.

Ephesians 1:2, "Grace be to you, and peace, from God our Father, and from the Lord Jesus Christ."

Ephesians 1:6-7, "To the praise of the glory of his grace, wherein he hath made us accepted in the beloved. In

173

whom we have redemption through his blood, the forgiveness of sins, according to the riches of his grace;"

Ephesians 2:5, "Even when we were dead in sins, hath quickened us together with Christ, (by grace ye are saved;)"

Ephesians 2:7-8, "That in the ages to come he might shew the exceeding riches of his grace in his kindness toward us through Christ Jesus. For by grace are ye saved through faith; and that not of yourselves: it is the gift of God:"

Ephesians 3:2, "If ye have heard of the dispensation of the grace of God which is given me to you-ward:"

Ephesians 3:7-8, "Whereof I was made a minister, according to the gift of the grace of God given unto me by the effectual working of his power. Unto me, who am less than the least of all saints, is this grace given, that I should preach among the Gentiles the unsearchable riches of Christ;"

Ephesians 4:7, "But unto every one of us is given grace according to the measure of the gift of Christ."

Ephesians 4:29, "Let no corrupt communication proceed out of your mouth, but that which is good to the use of edifying, that it may minister grace unto the hearers."

Ephesians 6:24, "Grace be with all them that love our Lord Jesus Christ in sincerity. Amen."

It is this preoccupation with the grace of God that makes our speech pleasant and tasteful to the lost ("seasoned with salt"). The lost need to hear of condemnation, judgment, wrath and hell, but grace and love give balance back to the nature of God. The only way these unfathomable truths can be adequately communicated to the heart of a lost soul is through the synergism that exists between the Spirit of God and a yielded Spirit-"filled" believer.

LEARNING TO BE A SPIRITUAL DIAGNOSTICIAN

Lastly, not every lost person should be approached the same way - "that ye may know how ye ought to answer." An answer presumes a question has been asked. All too often Christians begin to give answers before questions are asked. Just as different questions require different answers, so do people with different beliefs require different truths. Sometimes before we speak to the lost, we need to listen to them. We need to ask the right questions and listen carefully to their answers. We need to find out what they believe and help them take those beliefs to the Word of God for comparison. We need to *expose* the lost to truth of the Word more than just *telling it to* them.

Open the Scriptures to a selected verse that corrects their false belief. Have them read the verse out loud. Ask *them* what the verse means. Try to help them understand the meaning without telling them what it is (if possible). What a person discovers for himself is always more solidifying when it comes to his convictions.

Jesus is Lord!

Studies in the Epistle to the Colossians
Chapter Twenty-one
PUTTING SPIRITUAL FLESH ON OUR THEOLOGICAL BONES
(Living the Truth We Know)

1. Why is it important to understand that the break between chapters three and four in Colossians is really after 4:1?

2. What is the attitude of prayer? From that understanding, what is the meaning of the admonition "continue in prayer" in Colossians 4:2?

3. What does the word "watch" mean in Colossians 4:2?

4. What two things does the real prayer of faith expect? Why does it expect these two things?

5. Read Hebrews 4:14-16. Why should all believers live in constant praise and thanksgiving?

6. What does the word "withal" mean in Colossians 4:3? How does understanding this meaning effect your understanding of the rest of this verse?

7. What is meant by *focused* or *targeted* prayer?

8. *Targeted prayer* should go in two directions. According to Colossians 4:3-4 what are they?

9. What must a person *understand* before he can believe?
   A. How would you pray specifically for another Christian so this can be accomplished?
   B. How would you pray for the lost so this might be accomplished?

10. List the four responsibilities of the believer in living his life before lost people from Colossians 4:5-6.

Jesus is Lord!

Studies in the Epistle to the Colossians
Chapter Twenty-two
THE INTERDEPENDENCY
OF CHRISTIAN SYNERGISM

"[7] All my state shall Tychicus declare unto you, *who is* a beloved brother, and a faithful minister and fellowservant in the Lord: [8] Whom I have sent unto you for the same purpose, that he might know your estate, and comfort your hearts; [9] With Onesimus, a faithful and beloved brother, who is *one* of you. They shall make known unto you all things which *are done* here. [10] Aristarchus my fellowprisoner saluteth you, and Marcus, sister's son to Barnabas, (touching whom ye received commandments: if he come unto you, receive him;) [11] And Jesus, which is called Justus, who are of the circumcision. These only *are my* fellowworkers unto the kingdom of God, which have been a comfort unto me. [12] Epaphras, who is *one* of you, a servant of Christ, saluteth you, always labouring fervently for you in prayers, that ye may stand perfect and complete in all the will of God. [13] For I bear him record, that he hath a great zeal for you, and them *that are* in Laodicea, and them in Hierapolis. [14] Luke, the beloved physician, and Demas, greet you. [15] Salute the brethren which are in Laodicea, and Nymphas, and the church which is in his house. [16] And when this epistle is read among you, cause that it be read also in the church of the Laodiceans; and that ye likewise read the *epistle* from Laodicea. [17] And say to Archippus, Take heed to the ministry which thou hast received in the Lord, that thou fulfil it. [18] The salutation by the hand of me Paul. Remember my bonds. Grace *be* with you. Amen. *Written from Rome to Colossians by Tychicus and Onesimus*" (Colossians 4:7-18).

It can be said of the *ocean of souls* born again into the family of God, no person is an island unto himself. Each of us is a connecting link to another brother or sister in Christ. Each life touches the life of another positively or negatively for the cause of Christ. In this text we have a record of the positive aspects of this truth. What a sweet testimony of love and appreciation for one another. What a wonderful example of encouraging one another in the Lord.

We find in this text a number of examples of how believers are to minister one to another. We see a sweet harmony of lives focusing on edifying the *body of Christ*. There is a real interdependency of believers striving for a common goal. We see a group of believers laboring together in blessed fellowship even though some of these were in prison at the time.

We do not see the petty bickering that is evident in so many local churches today. We don't see a power struggle. We don't see any behind the scenes political manipulation. We just see each individual Christian doing whatever he could to help his brother or sister in Christ succeed in ministry. What a glorious testimony to the Lordship of Christ in the lives of these believers. What a contradictory testimony to the Lordship of Christ when these things are not evident.

TYCHICUS WAS A COMMUNICATOR OF NEEDS (COLOSSIANS 4:7-9).

Tychicus was an apostolic delegate used by Paul on numerous occasions to carry offerings and messages (*such as the Epistle to Colosse*) to other local churches. He communicated the needs of Paul and the other missionaries with him.

"And there accompanied him into Asia Sopater of Berea; and of the Thessalonians, Aristarchus and Secundus; and Gaius of Derbe, and Timotheus; and of Asia, Tychicus and Trophimus" (Acts 20:4).

"But that ye also may know my affairs, and how I do, Tychicus, a beloved brother and faithful minister in the Lord, shall make known to you all things" (Ephesians 6:21).

"Grace be with all them that love our Lord Jesus Christ in sincerity. Amen. To the Ephesians written from Rome, by Tychicus" (Ephesians 6:24).

"All my state shall Tychicus declare unto you, who is a

beloved brother, and a faithful minister and fellowservant in the Lord" (Colossians 4:7).

"And Tychicus have I sent to Ephesus" (II Timothy 4:12).

"When I shall send Artemas unto thee, or Tychicus, be diligent to come unto me to Nicopolis: for I have determined there to winter" (Titus 3:12).

PAUL'S COMMENDATION OF TYCHICUS (COLOSSIANS 4:7)

1. He was "a beloved brother."
2. He was "a faithful minister."
3. He was a "fellowservant in the Lord."

Do you suppose Paul and Tychicus ever had a disagreement in all the time they spent together? Do you suppose they knew each other's character flaws, spiritual weaknesses, and faults? Do you suppose Tychicus was without faults? Does Paul mention one of them?

When we find fault with a brother or sister in Christ (*and there will always be a when*), if we feel a need to communicate that fault, it should ONLY be with that brother or sister. When we focus on a person's strengths, we help him capitalize on those strengths. When we focus on a person's weaknesses and try to bring everyone focus there, we rob him of his potential in Christ and destroy his opportunity to minister successfully. Paul promoted Tychicus' strengths so that Tychicus could be the most effective in his ministry to others.

IT IS APPARENT FROM COLOSSIANS 4:10-14 THAT THIS WAS A GROUP OF BELIEVERS WHO REALLY LOVED AND CARED FOR ONE ANOTHER.

It is obvious these people shared a bond that is seldom seen in local churches today. Perhaps it was because they were so busy struggling to just stay alive and be effective that they had little opportunity to turn on one another. When we understand the dynamic of spiritual synergism and understand that we depend on one another for the survival of that synergism, we will tend to protect each other rather than devour one another. It is usually the Christian who is not involved in the struggle for souls who turns to attack one of his brethren. The greatest dangers in any local church are those who consider it their duty to criticize and evaluate all the other people in the church.

EVEN THOUGH ARISTARCHUS AND EPAPHRAS WERE IMPRISONED WITH PAUL AT ROME, THEIR MINISTRY AND CONCERN WAS STILL FOCUSED ON OTHERS (COLOSSIANS 4:10 AND 12-13).

The probability is that these two men voluntarily alternated in sharing Paul's prison cell, even though they were not required to be in prison. They really cared for Paul. Epaphras was with Paul when the church at Colosse, Laodicea, and Hierapolis were founded.

His love and concern for the people in these churches never stopped. Even though he was no longer their pastor, he continued to be genuinely concerned for them. They were more than fellow Christians. They were truly viewed as brothers and sisters in Christ. They were a loving, caring family whose love for one another was not minimized by the miles between them.

The family ties are evident in Epaphras' intercession for his brother's and sister's in Christ. Paul's testimony about Epaphras was he was "always labouring fervently . . . in prayers" for them, usually to the point of exhaustion. "Fervently" in Colossians 4:12 is from the Greek word *agonizomai* (ag-o-nid'-zom-ahee). It means to enter a contest such as contending in the gymnastic games, to contend with adversaries; to fight. Metaphorically it referred to a struggle with the potential of great difficulties and dangers.

Epaphras had "a great zeal" for these believers. He really wanted them to succeed in their ministry. But most of all he loved them with an overflowing heart.

"REMEMBER MY BONDS" (COLOSSIANS 4:18)

Paul (*and each of the men listed*) had invested their lives so that these believers could be saved and established in the faith. These men gave up much in life to preach the Gospel. Ministry is about sacrifice. Sacrifice is the measuring stick of love.

"[1] Am I not an apostle? am I not free? have I not seen Jesus Christ our Lord? are not ye my work in the Lord? [2] If I be not an apostle unto others, yet doubtless I am to you: for the seal of mine apostleship are ye in the Lord. [3] Mine answer to them that do examine me is this, [4] Have we not power to eat and to drink? [5] Have we not power to lead about a sister, a wife, as well as other apostles, and as the brethren of the Lord, and Cephas? [6] Or I only and Barnabas, have not we power to forbear working? [7] Who goeth a warfare any time at his own charges? who planteth a vineyard, and eateth not of the fruit thereof? or who feedeth a flock, and eateth not of the milk of the flock? [8] Say I these things as a man? or saith not the law the same also? [9] For it is written in the law of Moses, Thou shalt not muzzle the mouth of the ox that treadeth out the corn. Doth God take care for oxen? [10] Or saith he it altogether for our sakes? For our sakes, no doubt, this is written: that he that ploweth should plow in hope; and that he that thresheth in hope should be partaker of his hope. [11] If we have sown unto you spiritual things, is it a great thing if we shall reap your carnal things? [12] If others be partakers of this power over you, are not we rather? Nevertheless we have not used this power; but suffer all things, lest we should hinder the gospel of Christ. [13] Do ye not know that they which minister about holy things live of the things of the temple? and they which wait at the altar are partakers with the altar? [14] Even so hath the Lord ordained that they which preach the gospel should live of the gospel. [15] But I have used none of these things: neither have I written these things, that it should be so done unto me: for it were better for me to die, than that any man should make my glorying void. [16] For though I preach the gospel, I have nothing to glory of: for necessity is laid upon me; yea, woe is unto me, if I preach not the gospel! [17] For if I do this thing willingly, I have a reward: but if against my will, a dispensation of the gospel is committed unto me" (I Corinthians 8:1-17).

These men had given their lives for the cause of Christ. The recipients of this epistle *(and the others)* were their long term investment. Sometimes Christians forget, or take for granted the investment people *(pastors and missionaries)* have made in time and effort to bring them to Christ and lay the necessary spiritual foundations so they can live for Christ. We take for granted those missionaries who labor for a lifetime in some small city thousands of miles from their families.

God's calling binds them there as much as any prison cell. They went there to minister, trusting that God would provide for their needs. They trust God that He will raise up faithful people who will provide those needs. However, they will stay and do whatever is necessary because God has called them there. Christians need to "remember" that these people are "bondslaves" of Christ. They serve Him where ever He calls them, regardless of the sacrifices necessary because He is Lord and they love Him.

Jesus is Lord!

Studies in the Epistle to the Colossians
Chapter Twenty-two
THE INTERDEPENDENCY
OF CHRISTIAN SYNERGISM

1. Read Acts 20:4. What was Tychicus' relationship with the Apostle Paul? Do you suppose they knew each other intimately?

2. List Paul's three commendations of Tychicus in Colossians 4:7.

3. Do you think Paul was familiar enough with Tychicus to know his faults, failures and spiritual weaknesses?
   A. Does he mention any of them?
   B. Why not? Didn't these people deserve to know these things if he was going to minister to them?

4. What happens when we are able to focus others on another's strengths?

5. What happens to a person's potential for a successful ministry when we bring focus on their weaknesses?

6. Read Colossians 4:10-14. Why do you think these people shared a bond that is seldom seen in local churches today?

7. What is usually characteristic of a believer who spends all of his/her time criticizing or attacking other believers?

8. Read Colossians 4:12-13. What can we learn about Epaphras in that Paul commended him for the people he had brought to Christ and pastored even though he was quite a distance from them? Why did Epaphras pray so fervently for these people?

9. Read Colossians 4:18. What is Paul reminding these believers about by the words "remember my bonds" (compare I Corinthians 8:1-17)?

Bibliography

Alford, Henry. *Alford's Greek Testament, Volume III, Galatians-Philemon.* Grand Rapids, MI: Baker Book House, reprinted 1980.

Barnes, Albert. *Ephesians, Philippians and Colossians; Notes on the New Testament.* Grand Rapids, MI, Baker Book House, Twentieth Printing 1981.

Bruce, F.F. *Paul: Apostle of the Heart Set Free.* Grand Rapids, MI: William B. Eerdmans Publishing Co., Reprinted January 1983.

Carson, Herbert M. edited by Tasker, R. V. G. *The Epistles of Paul to the Colossians and Philemon,* Tyndale New Testament Commentaries. Grand Rapids, MI: Wm. B. Eerdmans Publishing Co., Tenth Printing 1980.

Clarke, Adam. *Adam Clarke's Commentary on the Bible.* Abridged by Ralph Earle, 1966. Kansas City: Beacon Hill Press, Fifteenth Printing, September 1984.

Dowley, Tim, Organizing Editor, Briggs, John H.Y., Linder, Robert D., Wright, David F., Consulting Editors. *Eerdman's Handbook to the History of Christianity.* Grand Rapids, MI: William B. Eerdmans Publishing Co., Reprinted 1987.

Earle, Ralph. *Word Meanings in the New Testament, Volume V.* Grand Rapids, MI: Baker Book House, 1977.

Eusebius, Translated by Williamson, G.A. *The History of the Church from Christ to Constantine.* New York, NY: Dorset Press, 1984.

Klimkeit, Hans-Joachim. Gnosis on the Silk Road: Gnostic Texts from Central Asia. San Francisco, CA: HarperSanFrancisco, 1993.

Lightfoot, J.B. and Harmer, J.R., Translators, Edited and revised by Holmes, Michael W. *The Apostolic Fathers, Second Edition.* Grand Rapids, MI: Baker Book House, 1956.

Robertson, Archibald Thomas. *Word Pictures in the New Testament, Volume IV. The Epistles of Paul.* Grand Rapids, MI: Baker Book House, 1931.

Peake, A.S. edited by Rev. W. Roberson Nicoll. *The Expositor's Greek Testament* edited by Rev. W. Roberson Nicoll, *Volume III.* Grand Rapids, MI: Wm. B. Eerdmans Publishing Co., reprinted November 1980.

Unger, Merrill F. *Unger's Bible Handbook.* Chicago, IL: Moody Press, 1979.

Unger, Merrill F. *Unger's Survey of the Bible.* Eugene, OR: Harvest House Publishers, 1985.

Vaughan, Curtis. Gaebelein, Frank E., General Editor. *The Expositor's Bible Commentary, Volume XI.* Grand Rapids, MI: Zondervan Publishing House, 1981.

Vincent, Marvin R. *Word Studies in the New Testament, Volume III, The Epistles of Paul.* Grand Rapids, MI: Wm. B. Eerdmans Publishing Co., seventh reprinting, 1980.

Wood, Leon J. A *Survey of Israel's History.* Grand Rapids, MI: Zondervan Publishing House, 1986.

Wuest, Kenneth S. *Wuest's Word Studies from the English Bible, Volume I.* Grand Rapids, MI: Wm. B. Eerdmans Publishing Co., reprinted January 1979.

Lexicons and Dictionaries

Theological Dictionary of the New Testament,
Ten Volumes
Edited by Gerhard Kittel and Gerhard Friedrich.
Translated and edited by Geoffrey W. Bromiley.
Wm. B. Eerdmans Publishing Co., reprinted
September 1983

Richards, Lawrence O.
Expository Dictionary of Bible Words
Regency Reference Library
Zondervan Publishing House, 1985

Thayer, Joseph H.
*Thayer's Greek English Lexicon of the New
Testament*
Baker Book House, Fifth Printing March 1980

Unger, Merrill F.
The New Unger's Bible Dictionary
Edited by R.K. Harrison, Howard F. Vos and Cyril
J. Barber contributing editors.
Moody Press, Revised and updated 1988

Vine, W. E.
*An Expository Dictionary of New Testament
Words*
Fleming H. Revell Company, Seventeenth
impression, 1966

**The Zondervan Pictoral Encyclopedia of the
Bible**, Five Volumes
General Editor: Merrill C. Tenney
Associate Editor: Steven Barabas
Zondervan Publishing House; Fifth Printing 1982

The Online Bible 7.0, Deluxe Edition

www.ingramcontent.com/pod-product-compliance
Lightning Source LLC
Chambersburg PA
CBHW052002090426

42741CB00008B/1511